# THE
## *Property Investor's*
# BUYERS GUIDE

## PETER MASTROIANNI

First published in 2016 by Major Street Publishing Pty Ltd
Contact: E I info@majorstreet.com.au; M I +61 421 707 983; W I www.majorstreet.com.au

National Library of Australia Cataloguing-in-Publication entry

| | |
|---|---|
| Creator: | Mastroianni, Peter, author |
| Title: | The property investor's buyers guide/Peter Mastroianni |
| ISBN: | 978-0-9945424-5-8 (paperback) |
| Notes: | Includes index |
| Subjects: | Real estate investment – Australia |
| | Real estate development – Australia |
| | Real estate development – Finance |
| | Investments – Australia |
| Dewey Number: | 332.63240994 |

Internal design by Production Works
Printed in Australia by Griffin Press

10 9 8 7 6 5 4 3 2 1

ISBN 978-0-9945424-5-8

# [ about the author ]

Peter Mastroianni has been involved in the property industry for the more than 13 years. Peter is the founder of The Buyers Guide, he champions the 'rentvesting' cause and is a co-founder of what will be Brisbane's first residential Managed Investment Scheme.

His first book *The First Home Buyers Guide* is an Amazon bestseller. Peter is also an Accredited Finance Broker and an active member and participant of Property Investment Professionals of Australia (PIPA), a not-for-profit organisation focused on helping and protecting consumer interests in property investment.

Peter has written this book to help others make S.M.A.R.T property investment decisions. It showcases the appropriate avenues through which people can build wealth through property. Peter is a firm believer that anyone can get a foothold on the property ladder when they know how.

For additional help, resources and to contact Peter directly please take the time to review **www.thebuyersguide.com.au** and **www.rent vesting.com.au.**

# [ contents ]

# [ preface ]

What is it about property that makes it so entrenched in the Australian psyche, playing on our emotions, desires and needs? Is it the prospect of prosperity? Or the ability to provide stability and a secure home life? Maybe it's something aspirational, in that it could allow you to move away from the 9 to 5 grind. The combination of all of these factors may even seem life-changing.

In reality though, it may appear impossible to achieve these results from where you currently stand. However, with an understanding of what is possible you can focus your attention on achieving success.

## Why is that the case?

Well, you just need to look at the evidence to appreciate that accumulating wealth through property isn't always out of reach. Take this for example: according to the Australian Tax Office (ATO) there are more than 1.8 million individuals who own rental property. Almost 13 million individuals lodge a tax return, which roughly equates to one in six people owning an investment property. If you dig a little deeper into the data, it indicates that almost 73% of people who own an investment property, just own one. Less than 1% own six or more investments (see Figure 1 below).

### Figure 1: Number of properties owned by percentage of property investors

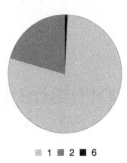

▨ 1 ▤ 2 ■ 6

There's nothing remarkable in those numbers until you discover that the vast majority of property investors have a taxable income of less than $80,000 a year, a third of whom have a taxable income of less than $37,000 annually (see Figure 2)!

### Figure 2: Annual assessable income of property investors

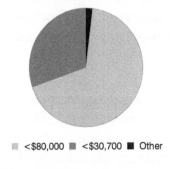

▨ <$80,000 ▤ <$30,700 ■ Other

Now, if you crunch the numbers behind these figures, the majority of these individuals are making a loss from their investments each year. I was taught that the goal of investing is to turn a profit, not make a loss. But these individuals are offsetting their losses against their taxable income and also anticipating long-term capital appreciation of their investments. And as we have seen more recently, that appreciation (or capital growth) is especially significant, albeit not in all markets.

These figures illustrate that buying an investment property doesn't require you to earn an annual salary of $100,000+. They do illustrate though that investing in property that is not your principal residence can be done on a much lower income. That being the case, why do the majority of Australians not invest in residential property? Well, the common factors are:

1. Risk – they resent the lifestyle sacrifices they may have to make.
2. Fear – of vacancy rates, bad tenants and interest rate movements, and they worry about stability in their employment.
3. Low-income – it is a perception that you need to be wealthy to invest. This is not the case; it is the ability to maintain a regular income that is imperative because you will need to borrow to buy.
4. Cash flow – the stress of covering additional expenses out of their wage puts pressure on the general household accounting budget.

Other concerns that prevent future property investors are many and varied. I mentioned fear above; a major hurdle is getting over the fear of making a dud purchase that will impact on your ability to generate or manufacture further equity. Making poor purchasing decisions is the number one killer of your ability to make a profit. Every investor will have a story about some of the bad choices they have made, but it's what they learn from those mistakes and how they follow up afterwards that determines their overall result. If you leave a bad purchase sitting vacant, making a loss and/or even reducing in value, you'll face a horrible outcome.

Some potential investors have the blinkers on. They focus too much on the short term – buying an investment property to make it into next year's tax refund. Then they hope for the market, area or region to 'pop' so they can immediately capitalise on growth. This is not a realistic strategy.

Another hurdle is not possessing the knowledge to invest wisely, not knowing what you're doing, not seeking professional advice. This, together with poor planning, will lead to poor to average results at best.

If you lack confidence, you're likely to do nothing, particularly if you've been burnt in the past. But sitting back and twiddling your thumbs will not produce results either.

## Reasons to invest in property

Now, to that smaller proportion of individuals earning less than $80,000 per year, what has forced their hand to make them take that leap into property investing? Common factors include:

- Property is a growth and stable investment.
- Property generates long-term income.
- Property can be seen, touched and altered to produce more growth and income.

And what has even a smaller proportion of the population done to build an asset base of three or more properties?

- They have bought below market value and continued to manufacture equity in the property.
- They have structured their loan facilities to work for them.
- They educated themselves to apply the right investment strategy suited to their needs and goals, to speed up the process of achieving their desired outcomes.

The success of some investors' portfolios is debateable. What's on paper and what the actual reality is can at times be poles apart. Significant house price increases over the past ten or so years have also shifted market expectations and the most traditional schools of thought towards achieving success in property.

The strategy, intention and desired result can at times get confused with reality. For example, a typical approach (one of which I'm guilty of myself and that applies to the old school of thinking) is:

- putting down a 20% deposit plus the required funds to cover purchasing costs;
- then paying market value to secure the in-demand property;
- renting the property out below market value to quickly attract tenants and generate some much-needed income;
- waiting for capital growth to create equity.

The problem with this approach is that you can find yourself waiting several years to produce a profit and even longer to make substantial equity to even consider purchasing your next property.

The alternative approach is to significantly sacrifice your lifestyle to scrape together another 20% deposit plus purchasing costs and make another purchase. This may only produce another loss, more ongoing expenses and it will impact your personal cash flow which stresses you out and traps you in your job and salary because you have invested yourself into a corner. This seems far removed from the lifestyle and success you had originally imagined, doesn't it? To break the cycle, you sell one property, pay tax on any capital gain, have a short holiday to say "job well done" and only actually realise a small profit. Upon reflection, you wonder if property investment is all it's cracked up to be.

Well, truth be told, it is, and it doesn't need to be as hard as the typical situation above which a lot of investors, all too commonly, find themselves in.

## The smart way to invest

S.M.A.R.T investors understand that there are ways to speed up the process. Understanding the different triggers that can be applied and developing a particular strategy that suits your risk profile, needs and desired goals will allow you to build your desired property portfolio much more quickly than you think possible.

S.M.A.R.T is the five-step process that you can apply to gain the essential knowledge, strategies and ideas to become the property investor that you want to be! The five steps are:

S   Steps to success
M   Managing the money
A   Accumulate
R   Risk management
T   Take off.

If you aspire to something more and have the resources – whether that be time, cash/equity or even just energy and motivation, then you're well on the way to becoming a S.M.A.R.T investor. This approach ignores passing trends and offers the potential for building a sustainable and balanced portfolio that will lead to property investment success, whatever that may look like for you!

This is the approach that I reveal to you the *Property Investor's Buyers Guide.*

# [ steps to success ]

Success will never be a big step in the future;
success is a small step taken just now.

**JONATAN MARTENSSON**

S.M.A.R.T investors take logical and purposeful steps to create their desired property outcomes. Their approach is methodical because of their implementation of well-crafted strategies. Property investment shouldn't be considered a side project, requiring a mad rush at tax time to gather documentation, tossed in with a property management dispute or two over mismanaged tenants. Fundamentally, it should be viewed as a business that has a structure, strategy and a plan. These three factors cannot be determined without knowing your 'why.'

The first step to success is knowing your why.

## DETERMINING YOUR 'WHY'

Doing anything without knowing or understanding why you are doing it is counterproductive. Investing in property is no different. In fact, not knowing your why is risky when investing in any asset class.

Therefore, ask yourself this question – why do I want to invest in property?

There are thousands of responses to such a broad question but when you boil it down it will be because of one of the four, or a combination of the four, factors shown in Figure 3 below.

### Figure 3: Four factors behind 'why' to invest in property

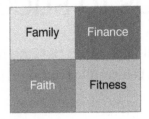

The four 'Fs' are intimately involved with one another. It's like a love square, where one might not necessarily know of the other, yet they all impact each other!

So what's your why? It could be one of the following:

- For property investment to better your family's situation?
- Because you have faith in your abilities to create something more in your life?
- Is it purely financial?
- Is it to create a lifestyle that would allow you to move away from full-time work, reduce stress and improve your health and fitness?

All these responses are interconnected, but some will have more meaning to you than others. Therefore, determining your why will influence your strategy. This is because it will impact on your willingness to take on risk, pursue alternative opportunities or even determine how much time, or when, you spend invested in the market.

## How to determine your why?

Simon Sinek has popularised the 'find your why' theme through his TEDx talk (the most watched in history). He believes you need to start with the 'why' to determine the 'how.' The why gives you a clue as to what you should do. This is particularly important when most of us have no idea what we are doing or why we do it for that matter. You may *know* what you want to do – but *why* is that?

I'm by no means an expert on finding the why so I thought it would be best to consult with Google. It's here that I stumbled across Mark Manson (**www.markmanson.net**) who outlines several strange questions that help you find your purpose. It's worthwhile asking these types of questions to give you an insight on your motivations for wanting to achieve success through property. Without further ado the questions are:

1. What is true for you today that would make your eight-year-old-self cry? What did you enjoy as a child that you loved but stopped doing because someone told you that you wouldn't be successful at it or that you would not make money from it?
2. How can you better embarrass yourself? People avoid embarrassing themselves, but to be good at something you initially start with no clue, embarrass yourself once, twice or more, before you learn and come good.

3. How are you going to save the world? There are lots of problems to choose from so what gets you riled up and wanting to make a difference? Find a problem and try and solve it.
4. Gun to your head, if you had to leave the house all day, every day, where would you go and what would you do? And don't choose anything that aligns with complacency. Passion is the result of the action, not the cause of it – and passion is a full contact sport.
5. If you knew you would die in a year from now, what would you do and how would you want to be remembered?

Finding one or two things that are bigger than yourself, getting off the couch and facing them head on is where the difference lies.

So where is your attention at?

Having determined your why can allow you to hone in on and create a strategy that will be fit-for-purpose – one that will allow you to move closer to your goals. The strategy you pursue will be the ultimate deciding factor in your pathway to success. The truth will always lie with the end result, so it is not a set-and-forget scenario. It requires patience, strategic tweaking when necessary, time and commitment.

What does success look like? Is success a $10+ million portfolio? Or is it just a simple holiday unit that provides good income returns or, better yet, is it solely for personal use?

Deciding what the result will be is a major factor in understanding and appreciating what you are working towards.

Knowing these factors then moves you to the second step to success which is being steadfast in your strategy creation and eventual pursuit.

## STRATEGY CREATION AND PURSUIT

When you know your why, pursuing it with passion can become a full contact sport. Good athletes will train night and day, be completely dedicated to their craft and protect themselves with headgear, mouthguards and even sunscreen and zinc.

Investing in property is no different. The knowledge you acquire is your training that you will eventually apply to your purchasing decisions. Knowledge will act as protection, along with a couple of other special tools we will mention in Chapter 4 on Risk Management. Success in competitive sport requires knowledge of the competition, your opposition's style, their methods of play and how to out-manoeuvre them. Investing in property is no different, in that to navigate your way around you need to know the market players that can help you execute your strategy. If you like, these are your 'coaches'.

The coaches who can help influence your strategic direction are listed in the table overleaf.

On your property investment journey, you will likely encounter all five of these professionals. Each has its own merits and personally I prefer to work with those who want to help provide solutions and understand your circumstances, rather than those making direct property recommendations. We discuss your investment team in more detail in Chapter 4 on risk management.

## Table 1: Property market players

| Profession | What They Do | Payment Method |
|---|---|---|
| Real Estate Agents | Sell new and existing properties and work on behalf of the vendor | Receive a sales commission from the vendor of between 1% and 3% |
| Project Marketers | Focused on high volume sales of new and off-the-plan developments | Remunerated by the developer and receive commissions of anywhere between 2% and 10% |
| Buyer's Agents/ Advocates | Work for the buyer to source, negotiate and secure property that meets their client's requirements | Various payment models exist depending on the service requirements. A full-service offering can be between 1% and 3% |
| Property Investment Advisers | Provide tailored strategic guidance on your property investment pathway | Again various models exist and they will be typically blended with other service offerings such as buyer's advocacy, mortgage broking or financial planning |
| Mortgage Brokers | Provide guidance on products and lending structures specific to your individual needs | Will receive an upfront commission (on average) of 0.65% and a trail commission of 0.11% of the loan value |

## STRATEGY CREATION AND SELECTION

Many Australians borrow significant amounts of money to buy a home and diligently meet the regular repayments for the next 20 or so years. There is nothing wrong with this, as paying off your home loan is an important piece of the wealth puzzle. However, solely doing this for the next 15 to 20 years will mean missing many other investment opportunities.

More often than not, it makes sense to establish other investment strategies while you're repaying your home loan, as you will benefit from the long-term potential growth of these investments. The problem then arises of making the right decision on the multiple property investment options on offer. Arguably, there is no right or wrong way when it comes to strategy selection; the strategy you choose needs to be tailored to you as an individual. Many investors make money no matter the stage of the property cycle, the approach they use or level of financial investment because of experience and expertise.

Historically, the Australian real estate market has shown incredible strength. However, volatility has played its role too and will remain an ever-present risk factor. To make the most of the market advantages requires planning, in-depth research and careful management. As an investor you should frequently review your objectives and adjust your plan, strategy and capital structure to remain one step ahead of new or potential market headwinds.

If you're starting out in property investment small steps are best. A large bet that goes pear-shaped early in the piece could have disastrous long-term effects, and could just as easily put you out of the game entirely.

Inevitably, a combination of tactics will be used at the same time. Hypothetically, your long-term strategy might be 'buy and hold', but in the short term you could undertake a strategic renovation to manufacture equity and positively gear the property (more about these strategies later). Another example could be to implement positive and negative gearing strategies because you are pursuing growth and income objectives. At the same time, you could be holding the assets through trust structures that allow you to minimise your exposure and transition gains/losses between the entities. Again, it all depends on your needs and circumstances as an investor.

Whatever strategy you feel is best, carefully assess yourself against the two Cs:

- capital; and
- capability.

Securing sufficient debt and manufacturing equity – i.e. getting enough capital – will be a continuous challenge. Loan structuring, serviceability, current regulatory reform and intervention in the market that could tighten lending policy all determine your capability. Plus, you need to consider your appetite for ongoing and increasing debt and risk.

> **DEFINITION**
>
> **Serviceability.** This is your ability to 'service' or meet the repayments on your loan. When a lender assesses your serviceability, they will consider your wage or salary, other income and other outgoings and liabilities.

Your capability, your partners and service-providers will dramatically influence potential results. If lending policies continue to tighten, securing lenders' support through the backing of an experienced and capable team can help sway decisions, particularly in your development-related activities.

The strategy direction you choose will be influenced by four key factors:

1. Your risk profile
2. Market factors
3. The timeframe available
4. Your growth, income and investment preferences.

You may have a solid existing plan but working through these factors and deciphering facts could result in necessary adjustments. Strategy selection is not a set-and-forget type of scenario. Your property investing strategy should be continually reviewed to take into account market directions and swings, along with changes in your personal situation which impact your previously selected direction and agenda.

If you want to pursue a more aggressive strategy, you may need to consider an 'active' property investment strategy, leaning towards shorter timeframes and more development-focused activity. Conversely, if it is growth and lower risk that you are after, a 'passive' strategy aligned to long-term ownership of blue chip stock might be more appropriate. These overarching strategies intertwine with the four factors above, and we will discuss these in greater detail later in the book.

## ASSESSING YOUR RISK PROFILE

Universally, investment risk consideration is given to tolerance, capacity and required risk (see Figure 4 below).

Figure 4: Risk profile considerations

Tolerance is related to your individual psychological characteristics, whereas risk required and risk capacity relate to the numbers of the actual investment. Ideally, you will obtain professional advice to understand the trade-off for each, so that you can reach an optimal solution as an investor. There is a big difference between moderate and very aggressive strategies, and your tolerance for risk will dictate the strategy that you ultimately pursue.

There are six risk profile categories (see Figure 5 below):

## Figure 5: Risk profile categories

1. Risk averse
2. Conservative
3. Moderate

4. Moderately aggressive
5. Aggressive
6. Very aggressive

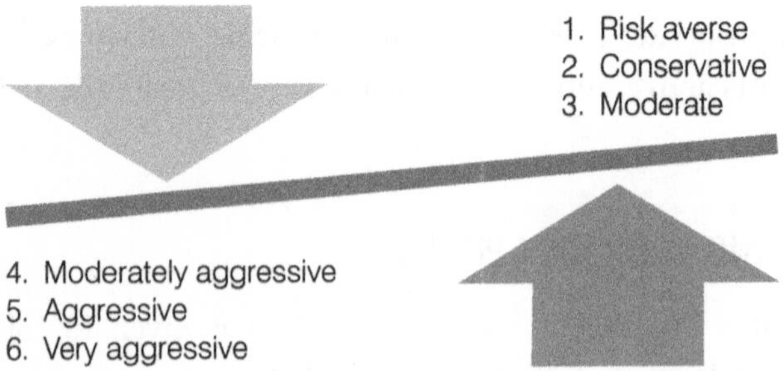

The arrows in Figure 5 correspond to the potential returns you can expect from your position on risk – i.e. lower returns can be expected from lower-risk strategies (1 to 3 above) and higher potential returns from high-risk strategies (4 to 6 above) – after all why would you be prepared to take the added risk? Note the word 'potential'; taking a higher risk does not mean higher returns are a certainty.

Risk tolerance is likely to have the most impact on your willingness to proceed with various ventures. The differing degrees of investment risk that an investor is willing, or can afford, to accept vary significantly from one person to the next. Risk tolerance is also affected by time-lines, future earning capacity and income from other assets.

If you are considering property investment, it is worth seeking professional advice to weigh up your investment options against the other asset classes. I'm 'pro' property obviously, but also I believe in balanced investing and maintaining the right mix of assets. Theoretically then, when one market is down, hopefully, the other portion of your portfolio is growing in another market. Diversity is like an offset account for risk.

However, as an overall asset class, property has historically proven to be far less volatile than the sharemarket for example. It also offers tax advantages and provides better leverage and is perhaps more predictable than shares. Advantages and disadvantages of investing in shares and property are given in Table 2 on the next page.

It is important to consider all available options seriously, and if you are risk-conscious, diversification will certainly help in reducing the volatility of your investment portfolio. You will need a plan for your investments that provides a framework for selection to balance affordability and growth against your financial goals. Regular monitoring, evaluation and consultation with your professional service-providers are also a must. Chapter 4 discusses risk in more detail.

### DEFINITION

**Margin call.** Buying 'on margin' means borrowing to buy. If you have borrowed to purchase a parcel of shares and the share price or overall market falls in value, your lender may demand a greater security to adjust the loan-to-value ratio. This demand is referred to as a 'margin call'. If you can't afford to pay this, you may be forced to sell the shares when you would otherwise choose not to do so.

Table 2: Comparison between investing in shares and property

| Investing in shares | | Investing in property | |
| --- | --- | --- | --- |
| Advantages | Disadvantages | Advantages | Disadvantages |
| Franked dividends | Brokerage costs | Significant tax benefits | Liquidity |
| Range of opportunities | Management fees | Capital stability | High entry and exit costs |
| High liquidity | High volatility | Low volatility | Bad tenants |
| Ability to reinvest dividends | Higher interest on borrowing (and more security needed) | No margin calls | Maintenance |
| Medium leverage possibilities | Possible margin calls | High leverage possibilities | Vacancies |
| Little correlation to property | Time-consuming if self-managed | Sector and location diversification | |
| Ease of diversification | | Government subsidies | |

## MARKET FACTORS

Over the long term, property prices have risen drastically, although the growth rate is far from consistent year-on-year. Generally, after extended periods of growth, the property market will take a breather, when prices will stagnate, or they may even drop a little, before increasing once again. Most forecasters believe this cycle takes somewhere between seven to eight years. In most cases, though, there is a short period when prices will increase sharply and in the remaining period not a lot tends to happen.

Broadly speaking, a lot of factors will impact property prices, including housing supply and demand, the economy, the ability to obtain credit and variances in government policy. Interest rates and population growth are two factors that can have a significant influence on property values' growth within specific regions.

Population growth in Australia has been steadily increasing, which puts pressure on housing supply. At the time of writing this book, there are record low-interest rates, so borrowing money is cheap and people have ploughed their money into property. This in turn influences growth.

Importantly, remember, property is not a one-size-fits all approach. Different markets, locations and pockets of the market can perform vastly differently to one another. Sydney and Melbourne showed stellar growth in 2015 when most of the rest of Australia merely plodded along (albeit some pockets in those markets did in fact boom).

Different areas go through various cycles, and it's important to ascertain whether the conditions favour the buyers or the sellers. Understanding where the current position of the property cycle sits can help influence your decision on where to buy, what asset to purchase, and potentially it could indicate whether values are likely to grow, stagnate or fall.

It can be like crystal-ball gazing, as market forecasting is difficult. Property prices do not always go up, they are like any other investment in that they go down as well. Time in the market is the true reason for the overall success of many long-term investors.

So why is it that prices fluctuate, but you hardly ever see a drop in real prices? Well, in a recovery market prices rise at a faster rate than inflation and therefore outperform in real terms. In a downturn, investors will tend to hold the asset rather than sell and realise a capital loss. The outcome of this is that a corresponding fall of some significance, in real prices, doesn't eventuate. Instead, prices flatten out or decline marginally as the sales volume falls, and the consequence is a smaller fall in real terms.

Short-term influences on the timing and the extent of change of the property cycle include:

1. Cost and availability of finance
2. Government policy
3. Economic environment.

The property cycle, influenced by broader economic, demographic and external factors, affects demand and supply. These factors all affect the market and, subsequently, prices.

There are four distinct phases of the property cycle shown in Figure 6.

**Figure 6: The four phases of the property cycle**

BOOM
– Shortage of trades
– More buyers than sellers
– Low rental yields and high confidence

RECOVERY
– Rentals increase
– Stock levels tighten
– Prices rise

SLOW DOWN
– Affordability crisis
– Stock oversupply
– Falling construction prices

SLUMP
– Abundance of trades
– Valuations fall
– More sellers than buyers

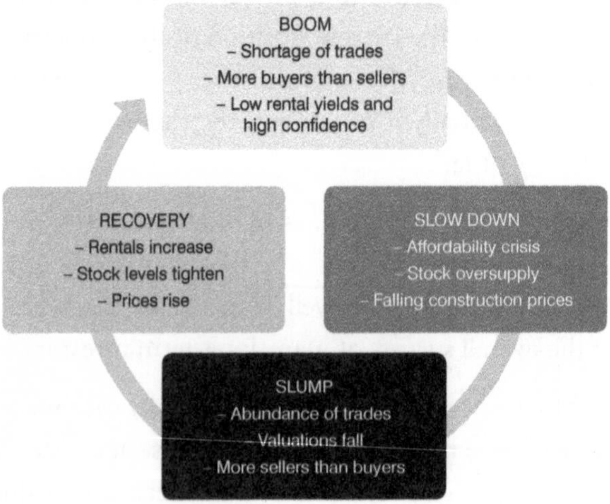

The four distinct phases are testament to the fact that prices do not always rise. Knowing where the property cycle is for the particular area you are targeting is a key consideration. Turnover of stock, or the volume of property traded due to the phase of the cycle, tends to favour the buyers or the sellers at that particular time. Cycles can vary in length from five to eight years and will be specific to each region. Just because the overall market sentiment is down, doesn't mean that there aren't hotbeds of activity around somewhere.

## TIMELINE AVAILABLE

Time is a critical factor in the success achieved through property investment. A mediocre purchase in the short term could make a strong recovery over time. Flipping a property, i.e. buying and selling in a short period, will dramatically decrease your holding costs and potentially increase your profit. Different strategies produce different results, but a commonality through all of them is time.

When developing your property investment plan, give careful consideration to the time you have available. Consider the time you have to achieve your goals and why you need that dedicated amount of time.

Property success comes over the long term, although a good purchase at the right time can quickly produce a profit. However, good investment-grade property can be difficult to obtain. Not all suburbs are investment grade, and not all properties in investment-grade suburbs are suitable. Therefore, asset selection becomes a critical success factor, even if it is time that ultimately produces results. Timing can be directly correlated to the property cycle.

However, if you are waiting for the perfect time to invest you probably won't do anything at all. Also, if you solely focus on purchasing below market value, you could be missing out on full priced properties that have better long-term growth prospects. This means that initial savings you may make of $20,000 will be inconsequential compared to the compounding 2% higher capital growth rate over the next ten years on a better investment-grade property bought for fair market value. Commonly, long-term property investors use two strategies:

1. Buy and hold
2. Investing through self managed superannuation.

## Buy and hold

Two words define this strategy and they are 'simple' and 'safe'. Property requires a significant investment of capital. Furthermore, there are significant entry costs and ongoing holding costs for property. True returns will usually start kicking in after seven or more years because of compounding capital returns. The longer the property is held then the greater the potential returns.

Holding on for the long term doesn't guarantee success, but it's a pretty realistic prospect. What works for investors is sourcing high-growth properties and also achieving the income needed to hold them. Hence why a strategy based on growth *and* income becomes necessary.

Holding property enables investors to ride the property cycle and sell when they feel the conditions are 'prime' or best suited to them. Timing the market entry point is important as you ideally don't want to be buying at the top of the cycle, because you'll need to sell at the top of the next cycle to achieve any kind of real growth. You avoid this error by careful market research which we cover later in the book.

If you hold property over the long term, the rental income is contributing to ongoing costs and growth, allowing you to claw back the purchase price and upfront costs through equity gains. Equity will become a very powerful tool in your investment toolbox as it will provide the means to build your property portfolio. Inflation too plays a role in that over time property prices and rental values increase, and your mortgage repayments will become comparatively cheaper, assuming debt levels remain the same. Tax advantages also play an important role in a buy-and-hold strategy.

Capital growth and yield work in conjunction with one another. Investing in high-potential capital growth areas can add significant passive wealth over the medium to long term. The rate of increase will depend on the type of investment purchased. Historically, those who stay in the game the longest will win. Time in most cases shapes the overall performance of your property portfolio. If you intend to pursue an active investment strategy and a shorter-term focus you need to consider:

1. Transaction costs
2. Capital gains tax (CGT) and the goods and services tax (GST).

## DEFINITION

**Capital gains tax (CGT).** Capital gains are the profits investors realise when they sell an asset for a price that is higher than the purchase price. Several methods are used to calculate CGT which vary according to the length of time the asset is held, always charged at your marginal tax rate. If the asset is sold within 12 months, full rates apply – over 12 months, a 50% discount would apply. Other variances affect this complex area of taxation. Clearly, it pays to have someone to help you navigate this taxation liability.

**Goods and services tax (GST).** Goods and services tax is a broad-based tax of 10% on most goods, services and other items sold or consumed in Australia. It is not levied on sales of residential property, however if you buy commercial premises, you may be eligible to claim a credit for the GST included in the purchase price.

Tax and costs can make a significant dent in the overall profit outcome of your property investments. In a lot of cases, these costs can only actually be recouped in the long term.

Warren Buffett, who is one of the world's richest men and arguably one of the greatest investors of our time, has a preferred timeline for ownership: forever. It's pretty hard to argue that he's incorrect when his accumulated wealth is over US$60 billion!

If you find a quality property, in a great location, purchase it below market value and hold it for the long term, you will hands-down be way ahead of any average investor who is scratching around for a 'deal.'

## Superannuation

Not being able to touch your superannuation until retirement means for most people it is a long-term investment. Therefore, if you want to pursue this strategy, you need to be comfortable with the timelines involved. If you're 35 years old and want to cash in on some investments in 10 years' time, perhaps to pay for your children's private high school education, then using super as your primary investment vehicle may not be the best option. Additionally, there are rules and limits to contributions you are allowed to make to your super, based on age.

It is possible to buy property through a self-managed superannuation fund (SMSF). However, most of us would find it difficult to purchase a property outright with the funds available in our super. In 2007, the rules changed around gearing inside super making it possible to borrow to buy property.

Since then, lenders have developed suitable lending products to meet the strict rules around SMSFs borrowing to invest in property. Property investing has taken off and is currently the fastest growing asset class held in super.

There are distinct advantages of investing in property through an SMSF, including the ability to combine balances of family members in the fund which increases the deposit you're putting down as well as keeps the fund positively geared.

Let's take a look at an example.

Nick and Clare are married and establish an SMSF combining their existing contributions of $80,000 and $150,000 respectively, totalling $230,000. Taking professional advice, they invest $130,000 in cash and shares. The remaining $100,000 they use to invest in a property – $80,000 for a deposit and $20,000 to cover upfront costs. They borrow $300,000 to fund the purchase of a $400,000 property. This rental property generates an income which is contributed back into the fund. Their employers continue to contribute 9.5% of their incomes into their super, which makes it possible for Nick and Clare not to have to make additional contributions to cover expenses. The result is a long-term, set-and-forget strategy with a potential positive cash flow effect.

Another sweetener in this scenario is taxation. Using the above example, if Clare's income were at the highest marginal tax rate, she would be taxed at 15% instead of 45%. This can be reduced even further by allowable deductions including depreciation on property. Capital gains tax will be a maximum of 10% per annum if the asset is held for 12 months or longer, and will reduce to zero if the property is sold when the fund is in retirement mode.

The final advantage of owning property in an SMSF is that it reduces the volatility of the portfolio because you are holding assets other than shares.

## Advantages of holding property in an SMSF

- Deposit and acquisition costs are paid using superannuation pre-tax monies.
- Rental income is taxed at 15% and not your marginal tax rate.
- You control what you want to invest in.
- There is another effective risk management strategy of holding life, trauma and income protection insurance with premiums paid with your super. Benefits also exist around estate planning and asset distribution.

There are some other factors to be aware of too:

- SMSFs are administratively intensive which means you pay high costs to run and maintain an SMSF.
- Not all property types are allowed to be held within an SMSF, and lending criteria, particularly around serviceability, are very different.
- SMSFs are regulated and operate in a heavily legislative environment that is under the watchful eyes of the government. Significant penalties apply to SMSF trustees not meeting the associated responsibilities and obligations. So if you are doing anything that contravenes the regulations – either knowingly or by mistake – be mindful that the consequences will be harsh!

**IMPORTANT:** If you are considering the benefits of establishing an SMSF, it's obligatory to seek professional advice from qualified professionals.

## INCOME AND GROWTH

The two factors that make property an attractive long-term investment are its ability to generate cash flow, or income, and capital growth. These two elements are not mutually exclusive and, in fact, are very dependent on each another. Focusing on growth will serve you well in the long term. However, it's likely you'll need healthy cash reserves to finance any shortfalls in servicing your loan(s). Pursuing income and sacrificing growth potential will mean a cash flow positive position but may fall short in the overall capital return stakes.

Growth versus cash flow is an actively debated topic, and a lot of investors focus on positive cash flow properties. However, it is quite likely you will need a combination of strategies to achieve your property goals. This means both cash flow positive and capital growth properties will be required in your portfolio. If you correctly structure your investments, you can have the benefit of moving profits and losses to your advantage. (I cover more about structuring later in this book.)

Gearing (or borrowing) is what makes this all possible, though. Very few investors have the funds available to purchase property outright. And if they do, it may not be the best use of capital. Borrowing money to invest in property or other asset classes is common place. Gearing is used by property investors as a wealth creation strategy and also for tax minimisation purposes. Negative gearing is a strategy that is used by many Australian property investors and positively geared investments are definitely in vogue too in the current low interest-rate environment.

As stated, a successful long-term property investment strategy will likely combine investing in both positively and negatively geared property. However, property results depend on the individual investor, and one strategy may be better than the other depending on your circumstances. For most regular investors who are looking to have more than one property in their portfolio, both types of gearing will most likely be required. Let's look at these in more detail.

## Positive Gearing

Positive gearing or investing in 'positive cash flow properties' is all the rage at time of writing. The hype is understandable, as by generating further income from property investing you have more extra income to be used to fund lifestyle requirements, pay down debt or grow your property portfolio.

Income is necessary, and it is even more important if your other earnings are moderate. The trade-off with cash flow positive properties is they tend to have lower capital growth over the long term. Capital growth is the aspect that generates real wealth over time. You may be lucky and find a cash flow positive property with exceptional capital growth potential. I refer to these as 'unicorns' – they are out there, but they're a rarity.

## Negative Gearing

Negative gearing is essentially the opposite to positive gearing, and it is beneficial in helping offset tax. Pursuing this strategy can trap moderate income-earners if they find themselves overexposed and leveraged too highly – be careful you can invest yourself into a corner!

The tax advantages associated with negative gearing are well known and they are the reason this strategy is so popular – everyone wants to minimise their tax. Negatively geared properties will also tend to favour long-term capital growth which could potentially make them more valuable than their counterparts over the long term.

Again, this is a strategy to implement in conjunction with positive gearing.

Unless, you have been hiding under a rock, you will be aware that negative gearing has received a lot of media attention in the run up to the 2016 Federal Election, with the Liberal and Labor parties at polar opposites on their respective policy stances. The Liberal/National Party proposed to keep negative gearing legislation as is, while the Labor Party proposed to legislate to reduce the tax benefits of the strategy should it come into power.

In my opinion, if either party had true gumption and tried to balance the budget and really get the economy firing, they would look at a whole raft of measures. Negative gearing should probably be among them, and superannuation, GST and social/welfare benefits also could be reviewed, and the list goes on.

Negative gearing is said to be a 'perk' of the rich. It's true that wealthy people do use it as a tax minimisation strategy, but so do many hard-working everyday Australians who are trying to take their financial security into their own hands. Most investors who negatively gear do so to get ahead in life, to fund their retirement or benefit the future of their families.

The recent (2015) boom in property prices can be contributed in part to negative gearing, it can also be attributed to record low interest rates, an underperforming stock market, baby boomers leveraging their SMSFs, foreigner investors, supply issues and many other factors. As a whole, they have all directly influenced demand and pushed up prices.

Despite the Liberal Coalition government's return to office in mid 2016, changes to negative gearing may still come but negative gearing will remain a relevant strategy in any property investor's toolbox. Sure it won't be the same but change breeds opportunity. The market will adapt and tailor products accordingly and it will move on.

We all know change is a constant and as investors we will see many future occasions where politicians will tweak, twirl and twerk their way around various policies. Hence, the importance on not setting and forgetting about your strategy. It should be regularly reviewed to take into account wider economic policy and what's also happening on the political front.

## A PASSIVE OR ACTIVE APPROACH?

Now, having decided upon a timeframe and gearing approach, the next decision to make is regarding going down a passive or active investment route. Here's what is involved with each:

1. Passive investors – favour long-term, lower risk, lower consistent returns.
2. Active investors – support short-term, higher risk, higher returns, i.e. development.

There is a third category and that is 'alternative investors' who consider new and emerging property investments.

Now let's explore the options that would be available under these broad categories.

### Passive Investment Approaches

Long-term investment decisions typically relate to a land banking scenario where you've secured property in a location primed for growth. Passive property-type options to consider would include:

1. Defence Housing
2. Residential property
3. Commercial property
4. Holiday/lifestyle property investments.

## 1. Defence Housing

Defence Housing Australia (DHA) is a government-run residential developer. It builds property for defence personnel and offers it back to investors in a leaseback arrangement which can last from three to twelve years.

> **DEFINITION**
>
> **Leaseback.** This is where you 'lease back' the purchased asset to the seller.

So what does DHA property have going for it?

- There's no vacancy risk as the DHA covers the rent during periods of vacancy.
- There are no management responsibilities. Coordinating tenants and taking care of the repairs and maintenance are all part of the deal. DHA will also refurbish the property when tenants move on too.
- Available stock tends to move quickly. Investors are attracted to the long-term security this offers.
- Being newly built, DHA property can be depreciated quickly.

What goes against it?

- A low-risk investment with few responsibilities comes at a cost. Yearly management fees are between 13% and 16.5% (which is high).
- Higher fees equate to lower rental returns. If you borrow money to invest, it could mean that holding costs are greater than for other property investment options.
- Location. Defence housing is built in areas suitable for defence personnel, which doesn't necessarily equate to a great location, and this can impact negatively on the capital growth potential.

- DHA properties are concentrated in the area as well. They are large in number, and the quality can be basic. Having lots of the same thing, of a low quality, in the same place, again won't favour capital growth.
- Little flexibility. You cannot improve the property to try and manufacture equity, nor can you increase the rent.
- When you sell, you are selling to another investor. Owner-occupiers will tend to pay a premium if it's something they want, whereas investors aim to negotiate the price downwards and can use location, quality and volume comparisons to support their offer.

In conclusion, significantly reducing risk, responsibility and running expenses comes at the cost of reduced yield (due to high management fees), and the capital growth potential can be weak. These downsides mean less profit is achieved. There's always a catch, isn't there?

Suitability of Defence Housing will depend on your risk appetite and return objectives. But when we are talking 'passive' this is about as passive as property investment gets.

**NOTE:** Throughout 2015 there was speculation that the federal government was looking closely at this scheme and rumour has it, it's earmarked for privatisation. Time will tell.

### 2. Residential property

It's what people know, like and trust. We grow up in it, entertain there, live our lives and raise our families there and use it as a vehicle to generate wealth and secure our future. Yep, it's good old-fashioned residential property – the darling of the property industry.

So what's the attraction? Let's take a look:

- Low volatility
- Tax advantages

- Capital growth
- Income
- Demand.

The downside of residential property centres around the high cost of entry, and it's not exactly a liquid asset. There is also the risk of buying in the wrong location and facing the real danger of your property's value stagnating or, worse, decreasing.

Demand for residential property will likely always remain strong, not only for owner-occupiers but also investors, because of the familiarity with the asset class. It is easily understood and people will invest in what they know and are comfortable with – and here lies the true beauty of the asset class.

Now you can investigate and dig out various numbers, statistics and charts and compare the difference between property and shares. Each will vary and tell a different story. If you pull data from 2013, it will indicate that shares have been the stronger performing asset class. If you pull data from today (2016) the reverse is true, as you'll see property has outperformed shares for the past ten years. It's important to note that both investment classes achieve the best gains over the long term. With some property, you can get lucky and snag a good buy, flip and turn it around for a quick profit. However, in most cases, property performs best when it is held for 7 to 10+ years.

**DEFINITION**

**Leverage.** This term is interchangeable with 'gearing'. Both terms mean to use other people's money (i.e. borrowed funds) to increase their returns.

Leverage is a powerful tool to build wealth and is put to best use via investing in residential property. Leverage through bricks and mortar has been the secret to the baby boomers' success as investors. The beauty is that you can borrow more when you use property as security compared to using a share portfolio. In the past, lenders have provided finance up to 95% of the value of property, whereas they may only lend 50% against a particular share or stock portfolio. This borrowing power allows you to benefit from the capital growth of a larger investment.

Manufacturing equity is another viable option for residential property investors. This can be achieved by adding value by renovating and making improvements. A well-timed strategic renovation can significantly improve the value of a property. These kinds of choices are all available because you have 100% control over the asset. You can influence the asset's overall worth and cash flow, depending on what you do and don't do.

While entry costs to property investment are high, they can become a tax deduction, as the revenue received from property can be offset against those costs and contribute to the reduction of the mortgage. Over time, the asset will pay for itself and bring you a revenue stream in retirement (if desired). Or it can remain an asset to pass on to future generations.

The beauty of property is that it's tangible, you can touch it, feel it, drive by it and know that it's safe. These factors alone give a lot of comfort to investors which are needed, from an emotional perspective, considering the large sums of money involved.

### 3. Commercial property
Demand drives capital growth in the commercial property space, with demand directly linked to economic growth. Historically, this has meant that the commercial property market is far less predictable than residential markets. There can be longer vacancy periods and poor resale value for some specialised assets.

Commercial property assets are held in a similar manner to residential property, i.e. they can be owned by individuals, companies, syndicates and trusts. Holding commercial property in an SMSF can provide investors with real benefits, particularly if the trustees are self-employed. A self-employed trustee can set up their SMSF, purchase a commercial asset which would be suitable for their business operations, and then rent it to their own business. There are significant advantages in this type of arrangement.

---

### Main differences between residential and commercial property

- Leases are longer but vacancies between tenancies can also be longer.
- Maintenance costs are usually covered by the tenant which means net income can be higher.
- GST is applied to the rent received along with any expenses relating to the property, including rates, water and other costs. You can claim the GST back as an 'input tax credit' against GST charged on the property's rent.

---

There are the following issues with commercial property also to consider:

- **Location.** Access to transport, visibility and surrounding businesses is vital.
- **Infrastructure.** Investigate future development potential in the area as it will either have a positive or negative impact on the property value.
- **Tenant quality.** A stable government or corporate tenant with a long lease is on the wish list of every commercial property landlord. Most importantly, consider the financial strength of the tenant and their potential longevity.

- **Building quality.** The overall quality and condition of the property will obviously impact your return.
- **Yield.** Rental reviews must be aligned to CPI or be incremental, and who covers what outgoings (the tenant or the landlord?) will have a bearing on the overall yield achieved.

More recently, commercial property has gained in popularity as investors are chasing security and income. Properties that attract blue chip tenants linked to long leases are in high demand. Established franchises such as Red Rooster, KFC, Hungry Jacks, BP service stations, Bunnings, etc., are all very attractive investment prospects, because in these cases the average annual after-tax return over ten years will be more than 10%, and much higher when you factor in capital growth.

### 4. Holiday/lifestyle investments

Who doesn't want to have a property at the beach? It's the dream of all investors.

The trouble with this scenario is that it boils down to buying with your heart as opposed to your head. It is important to understand how holiday rentals work and that the income they produce will fluctuate. Peak rental demand may only last for 8 to 12 weeks per year and depend on location, views, property quality and management – all are factors that influence vacancy rates. Volatility in this sector can be higher as holiday homes are expendable assets – they are one of the first to be divested if an owner starts experiencing financial hardship.

Finance policy relating to lending on holiday home property has slightly different loan-to-valuation ratio (LVR) requirements. Typically, the LVR will be lower than what is required to purchase a standard residential property.

Tax can be a little more complex if you maintain the holiday home as a rental for only part of the year. The reason is that you need to convince the Australian Tax Office (ATO) that the 'purpose' of the property is as a genuine investment. If this is accepted, you may be able to claim deductions such as interest expenses, but they will need to be pro-rated against the time the property was rented out and the time it was available for personal use. Capital gains tax will also apply upon the sale of the property.

The consistency of cash flow generated by holiday rentals can be the real issue. If you're a first-time investor and you need consistency, it may be better to consider alternative investments. On the other hand, if you're a wise old dog looking to diversify and lifestyle factors are an important consideration, then a holiday 'home' could well be worth considering.

So to have a 'home' away from 'home' that generates some income is great. Just remember the trade-offs could include long periods of vacancy and tax issues relating to the wear and tear on your possessions as the various short-term renters pass through.

## ACTIVE INVESTING – DEVELOPMENT

An active approach towards property investing will favour shorter terms, higher risk and higher potential returns. When we speak of an 'active' strategy, what we are referring to is development. This could be in the shape of a 'six-pack' type townhouse complex, a multi-level apartment building or merely a renovate-and-flip type project. The methods, strategies and opportunities for development are various, but there are some absolutes to cover. The main opportunities undertaken in the development space are:

1. Renovation
2. Subdivision
3. Development
4. Joint venturing
5. Land banking
6. No-money-down deals.

So let's get to it.

Development is an active approach to property investing as you're out in the market finding sites to do 'deals,' by turning property over quickly for a profit. This is different to the passive style of property investing, when investors hold property for an extended period, hoping the capital growth in the property will pay off or reduce the debt. The issue with this scenario is that interest rates have been higher and rental yields have been lower, so property may have been negatively geared which means that you may have been losing money while holding on to the property, which drags down your return.

At the moment, interest rates are at historic lows, and yields are relatively high. So, the reverse is taking place.

Development carries risk so you have to consider where your risk profile sits. If you have a low risk profile, you're better off choosing a safe, lower-return type of asset.

The first thing to build is a development strategy, followed by putting into place the right structure that will work specifically for you.

### Considerations when selecting how to structure investment property

- The tax payable on profits
- Your ability to access the property for private use
- Ability to access capital gain tax concessions
- Access to any losses made
- Personal liability exposure.

The right strategy will create tax efficiencies but you have to ensure that you don't get caught out. You could face a tax bill of $100k, plus fines and interest charges if you have relied on misinformation, or on a loophole that was incorrectly applied. If you're in the middle of a development project when this occurs, it will create problems because the bank will be chasing you for its money, your family will be worried, and the future of the project could end up on a knife's edge.

There are liability issues to consider as well – people do get sued, not often, but it does happen.

If you know and feel that property development is your pathway to success, you need to pass through several gates, and at each there is the potential for a misstep. Property development isn't undertaken by the masses because it can be overwhelming. Those who are not overwhelmed need to be confident that they have gained the knowledge, after undertaking thorough research, and have the planning skills necessary, otherwise mistakes will ensue.

If you have $200,000 in cash or equity, you can get started in property development. Mind you, on top of this figure you will need an ongoing income to service debt before income from the development comes on stream. To get around this, you could invest as part of a syndicate or joint venture, or you could undertake your own smaller development. Again, it depends on what intelligent and creative development strategies you can implement to increase your wealth position.

Whatever strategy you pursue there are five main gates that you will proceed through.

## 1. Advice and planning

The following should be part of your planning process:

- Get your house in order! Obtain asset planning and strategic guidance on the appropriate avenues to pursue.
- Creation of personal and investment budgets. Carefully assess current income streams because you will require a sustainable surplus. On the investment side: what are the costs? How will they be paid? What are the risks?
- Define what you want from the property and in what timeframe.
- Tax planning considerations and preparation.
- Obtaining the right finance requires an in-depth analysis of loan structuring and product selection. Ultimately, you'll want to reduce inputs and maximise returns.
- Consider doing projects under residential finance or obtaining loans based on the future value of the property, when the development has been completed.
- Time. Understand the best and worst-case timeframe scenarios and the effects each would have on your project and financial return. Do in-depth feasibility studies based on alternative time forecasts. You need to understand what you are embarking on and also appreciate the potential day-to-day impacts.

## 2. Site acquisition

Finding investment-grade sites is difficult, and if your current approach is to scroll through realestate.com.au listings, then you may have to find a new strategy. Good sites are rare and extremely competitive to secure, so sourcing can be complicated. You will need to develop connections, negotiate on off-market transactions, prospect directly and run the appropriate analysis on each opportunity before closing out the deal.

You need to be ready to act immediately when a suitable opportunity arises. It is imperative that you can be quick to take action, or else you'll lose the opportunity to someone better prepared. Have your finances in place and have access to specialists to undertake quick due diligence. Due diligence involves working through a lot of detail and gaining knowledge, so use professionals such as a town planner to look for imposed conditions, other current development assessments (DAs) or surrounding sites, as well as location and utility services. Ideally, professional advice is not something you want to penny pinch on.

No two sites are ever the same; they will all have their little peculiarities. Be aware of this from a site-risk perspective and choose sites that suit your strategy and budget.

Feasibility again needs to be undertaken on the site to make sure it is suitable. Have a detailed survey conducted so the draftsman/architect and builder can commence as soon as approvals have been handed down. A geotechnical report will indicate soil quality and ultimately have a bearing on the engineering for the slab and footings.

## 3. Development and planning

Development and planning tasks include:

- Having in place your specialist team, comprising a project manager (unless you plan to do this yourself), architect, town planner and engineer.
- Lodging your development application (DA) and building application (BA) and having them approved. The BA is a particularly detailed process, and you will require an engineer and architect to complete this part of the process.

## 4. Construction

When you reach the construction gate, you need to carry out the following tasks:

- Call for tenders
- Renovate, detonate or remove the existing dwelling
- Carry out groundworks
- Start construction
- Undertake ongoing management of time schedules and cash flow.

## 5. After development

Once the development is complete there is still work to be done, including:

- Sales or property management, depending on whether you are disposing of, or holding, the assets.
- Taxation! You need to understand your GST and CGT obligations. Again, this should have been completed during the planning stage.
- Estate planning.

You face numerous costs at each of these five stages of the development process, and it is imperative that you maintain a cash flow schedule and balance sheet.

Property development can be a risky exercise, but these risks can certainly be mitigated and managed. You do this by ensuring your team has the essential experience and expertise that aligns with your strategy. Find sites that suit your strategy, rather than a strategy that suits the site. You could come unstuck pursuing a strategy you're not familiar with, or you could over-leverage yourself. Ensure you have completed a robust feasibility and don't be afraid to fire someone if they are letting the team and project down. If you don't, it will only impede on the end results achieved.

Also, buy property with the right zoning for your strategy, that way you won't have to stress too much about not getting the DA. Timelines for your project will vary, but allow for a minimum of 12 months for a small development site – 18-months and longer timeframes are not uncommon, particularly for larger developments.

## YOUR PROFESSIONAL TEAM

The professionals whom you work with can make or break your property deal. You won't require the full team on each occasion but it's quite likely you'll need at least one, two or more of the service-providers listed in Table 3 overleaf on each occasion.

## TYPES OF DEVELOPMENT

There are some creative and intelligent strategies that people implement to generate wealth. The strategy that you pursue will depend on your risk tolerance, equity or cash position, time and resources available. Each plan will vary in complexity and detail. The higher the

**Table 3: Your team of property service-providers**

| Service provider | Who to select | Tasks |
|---|---|---|
| Lawyer | Property law specialist. | Contracts<br>Disputes and litigation<br>Structuring<br>Estate planning and risk management |
| Accountant | Property specialist. Don't just use the accountant who lodges your tax return unless they have particular expertise. Better yet, select accountants who are active property investors themselves. | Tax planning<br>Structuring<br>Risk management |
| Town planner | Someone who can demonstrate recent specific examples of achieving and implementing what you are trying to create. | Obtaining the Development Assessment<br>Liaising with council<br>Drafting and surveying (if they can offer these affiliated services) |
| Engineer | Specifically with a residential and commercial building background. There's no point appointing your mate who is a rail engineer. | Helping with the initial civil works<br>Helps obtain the Building Assessment |
| Architect | Again, make a choice based on past work and relevance to what you want to create. | Designs the dwelling concept to required standards and helps obtain the Building Assessment |
| Finance broker | If you are developing, seek a development finance broker. Alternatively, if you are a straight investor, choose a qualified broker with expertise in loan structuring. | Obtaining finance<br>Loan structuring |

complexity, the more variables and therefore, potential risk, which can be offset by a greater return. Common strategies include:

1. Renovation; and
2. Subdivision (combined with residential development. e.g. house/townhouse/unit/s).

Under these broad categories, many methods can be applied to spin a profit, manufacture equity and build wealth, which we will now explore.

## Renovation

The renovation strategy has a lot going for it because there aren't any barriers to entry, it can be relatively low risk, there are only moderate costs required and turnaround times can be quick.

Renovation can:

1. Manufacture equity if you intend to hold the property; and/or
2. Increase capital if you flip it (i.e. buy, renovate and sell within a short timeframe).

If your intention is to buy and hold property, then a strategic renovation could be an excellent approach. If it is done right, rental yields increase and equity in the dwelling should increase, and this can be put to use to fund the purchase of another investment.

---

### Important considerations as part of your planning process

- The structural integrity of the property.
- Does the intended renovation require any special approvals?
- Will the renovations appeal to a broad base of potential renters?

- Are the improvements adding value to the property without over-capitalising?
- Will the body corporate/owner's corporation (if applicable) impose any special terms or conditions?
- How are you intending to finance the modifications?
- What tax advantages (if any), including depreciation, can be claimed?
- How long will the renovation take? Do you have sufficient cash flow to cover the renovation and the period of vacancy?

When the renovation has been completed, remember to have the property revalued to improve your equity position.

An increasingly popular way to build equity and improve cash flow (in some states) is to build a granny flat at your property. (Obviously, this would only be a suitable option for a detached dwelling – I think you might be hard pressed to get the body corporate to approve a granny flat on common property.)

Granny flats can be delivered 'flat-packed', they are relatively inexpensive and can be built within a week. 'Demountables' or 'Dongas' (as they are commonly referred to in the mining industry) make great prefabricated homes in your backyard. Pending planning approval, you could pick up a flat pack from China for less than $10,000, or source it domestically from $80,000 and upwards. Installation and build costs are additional of course.

Granny flats can allow you as a property investor to earn higher or multiple incomes from the one property. This extra cash flow can sometimes be enough to turn a negatively geared property into a positively geared one. From a renter's perspective, it doesn't suit everyone. Some tenants will be bothered having to share with another potential stranger. Other tenants will see a granny flat as a positive –

for example, a family with an adult child still living at home but keen to have their own space.

'Flipping' is a commonplace strategy, as arguably 'flippers' are more readily available compared to investment-grade development sites. Flipping involves buying a property at the right time, holding it in the short-term and selling in a rising market. During this period you don't renovate but you may make cosmetic changes. It is the lower risk and moderate capital injections that make flipping appealing. Also, you don't have the worry of obtaining DAs and going through protracted council approval processes – unless of course you are undertaking major structural changes and extensions.

Risks associated with flipping properties centre on time because of holding costs if you miss the mark and can't sell within your time-frame. You have to be careful not to overpay for the property initially, and also not to overcapitalise on any improvements you make to it. Other risks include not properly identifying the demographics of the region, poor timing, the list goes on.

Cash flow is a key consideration and accurate cash flow projections are necessary to ensure a profitable outcome from you strategy. Again, obtaining the necessary approvals and complying with the regulations are essential. There are costs associated with purchasing and selling property and there may be tax to be paid and all these can add up to considerable amounts. But by sticking to a few rules you should still be able to secure a profit by:

1. **Buying below market value** – ideally, you want to purchase 20% or more below market value for property in the area. To achieve this, you'll need to 'sniff out' motivated vendors.
2. **Upgrade and up-style FAST!** The dwelling will need to have street appeal, along with nice big-ticket items such as a modern kitchen and bathroom. Doing anything structural

can blow out costs, so it is best to stick with existing layouts. A paint job, new carpets/tiles/polished floors, new blinds, fittings and fixtures will make a dramatic cosmetic improvement, which is all that you're after. You can do-it-yourself (DIY) if you have the time and capability. Otherwise, it may be better to outsource these improvements and project management instead. Styling the property when it comes time to put it on the market will improve the overall look and feel further and maximise the end sales result.

3. **Source properties at the low to medium end of the market.** This is because there is a larger pool of potential buyers to target when you come to sell, and secondly it is less risky due to the capital outlay. Renovations should meet market expectations. You may not need to install ducted air-conditioning, granite benchtops and brass bathroom fittings, as this may be over-capitalising in a market where you can reasonably expect sales of $450,000 to $500,000.

4. **Build a reliable team of tradespeople** around you and organise for them to commence work upon settlement or shortly afterwards. Remain front of mind with real estate agents in your preferred locations, as they could well end up approaching you with your next ideal project.

5. **Be realistic with your numbers.** Conservative figures are always best in these circumstances. Maintain a budget and cash flow statements, focus on the numbers.

Easily completed DIY improvements that are relatively cheap but make a vast improvement to the look and feel of a property can be completed to the exterior, and include:

- Holding a working bee! Round up the crew to weed, mulch, mow, fertilise, prune trees and bushes and dispose of any general items. Planting flowers to add some colour will naturally help dress things up.

- Using a gurney to wash the exterior of the house – this is a cheaper alternative to repainting.
- Selective painting – depending on the condition of the property you may be able to get away with just painting the gutters and trims and this will still make a big difference.

On the interior of the property you can:

- Clean and declutter to better present your property.
- Add a lick of paint that will make a significant improvement, not only in the look and feel but also the cleanliness.
- Use light to brighten up appearances for a more inviting feel. Replace old/dated light fittings and fixtures, including light switches. Open the windows and leave the lights on when you are presenting an open house.
- Replace curtains or blinds to dress up windows.
- Get the pest man out to get rid of spiders and insects.
- Repair, replace and renew low-cost fixtures and fittings to bring the property into the 21st century, e.g. door knobs, splash backs, change the toilet seat, etc.
- Stage the house with hired furniture for the professional photos and the open house. This does cost a bit, but it makes a significant impact, which is what counts if you intend to sell.

Is there are better strategy? Well, it just depends.

Property that is appropriate for flipping and making a good profit can be hard to find, but it can be worth the effort to realise profit in the short term. Holding property allows for the multiplier effect of buying, renovating and renting out and so it is probably a safer and more profitable strategy. Again, it just depends on the strategy you wish to implement. The big thing to remember about selling is that it is expensive. You've already paid borrowing costs, legal and stamp duty costs upon entry, and when you sell you have agents' costs, there may be capital gains tax (CGT) to pay and when you purchase again you'll be hit with stamp duty, legal fees, etc. again.

> **TIP:** Once you define your strategy, the best thing to do is find opportunities or 'deals' that suit, rather than find projects and then develop a concept to suit that particular project.

## Subdivision

Subdivision involves more complexity, risk and time but the rewards are potentially greater. If you are planning on using subdivision as a strategy you will need to proceed through a five-stage process:

1. Advice and planning
2. Site acquisition
3. Development and planning
4. Construction
5. Post-development procedures.

Very broadly these will be the gates you will need to proceed through during the subdivision process but, like all things, variances occur. Two main subdivision strategies involve:

1. Acquiring the site, stripping it or moving the existing dwelling to one portion of the block, and obtaining the DA for a concept development. Then you have the choice to sell it off for someone else to complete the construction; or
2. Acquiring the site, moving the existing dwelling or clearing the block, obtaining approval, developing yourself, selling the dwellings or holding (one or more) to rent out.

Numerous activities can take place between these two options and the variations primarily sit with construction. Again this will be defined by your strategy, concept, planning and site requirements.

Legislation and rules do vary considerably from state to state and council to council across Australia, so it is vital to consult with planning experts in the particular location where you are looking at subdividing. For a generic overview of a subdivision process the steps are presented in Figure 7 overleaf.

If you own the property, and it meets the criteria listed in Table 4 below, you are off to a good start. Alternatively, you will need to search and complete the due diligence to find suitable sites which meet these minimum criteria.

### Table 4: Minimum selection criteria when sourcing property for subdivision

| | |
|---|---|
| **Close to public transport** | • Schools and education in the area<br>• Retail and lifestyle facilities close by<br>• Suitable total area<br>• Appropriate usable area |
| **Suitable topography** | • Suitable vegetation<br>• Soil is conducive to building<br>• Low risk of stormwater |
| **Good local services** | • Not too much local traffic<br>• Low noise level<br>• Close to services and infrastructure<br>• Adequate waste collection<br>• Notations on the title |
| **Statutory authorities** | • Meets zoning regulations |
| **Clear title** | • No restrictive covenants or easements |

## Figure 7: Steps in the subdivision process

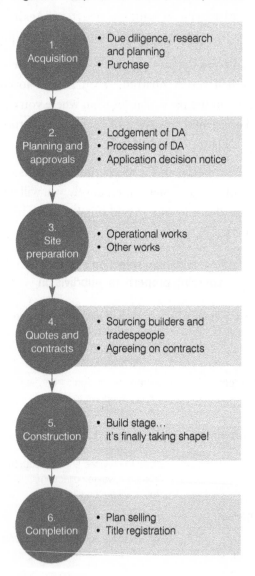

**1. Acquisition**
- Due diligence, research and planning
- Purchase

**2. Planning and approvals**
- Lodgement of DA
- Processing of DA
- Application decision notice

**3. Site preparation**
- Operational works
- Other works

**4. Quotes and contracts**
- Sourcing builders and tradespeople
- Agreeing on contracts

**5. Construction**
- Build stage... it's finally taking shape!

**6. Completion**
- Plan selling
- Title registration

Broadly, these criteria fall into the following five categories:

1. **Zoning.** This is a key consideration as the 'zoning' will define the legal and prohibited use of the land.
2. **Lot size.** Minimum square meterage will apply for different development and zoning purposes.
3. **Restrictions.** Aspects such as flood-prone land, stormwater development, waterways, soil quality, native vegetation, heritage, plus many others could limit or restrict development potential.
4. **Overlays.** This is a map indicating unique characteristics relevant to government or public interests relating to development. Overlays include features to protect, matters to consider and valuable resources. If the site falls in an overlay, there may be additional requirements to meet.
5. **Infrastructure.** Planned infrastructure developments could limit the use of the proposed development.

After obtaining this information and identifying a suitable site, it would then be appropriate to consult with a qualified planner.

Getting planning approvals through the relevant local council can be a time-consuming process. Applications need to be made within specified guidelines. This part needs to be spot on. You don't want the council to knock back your application because it is not in the required format or to their standards. This can cause substantial delays or the forfeiture of part, or the whole, application fee. That's why it is important to work with a town planning professional rather than tackling this yourself. Planners will also negotiate with the council on your behalf and follow up on the application status. Once lodged, the council will issue an acknowledgement which is relevant because the date of the acknowledgement provides the guidelines to the council to process the application within a certain timeframe (e.g. within six months of application). Again, this timeframe does vary from council to council.

Once the council is satisfied that your development will meet their requirements and the relevant legislation, they will issue the Decision Notice, which will include conditions. This approval will usually be valid for anywhere between 24 to 48 months, depending on the approval. This notice is essentially the Ts & Cs (terms and conditions) document that outlines the conditions that need to be met to settle the development within the specified time.

The next significant milestone will be completion of operational works that include clearing the block, earthworks, water, sewer, stormwater and electrical connection. An engineer will need to assist you during this stage to design and draft the proposed plans. These plans will require lodgement, and a separate charge may apply.

When you have progressed to clearing the block you may need to demolish structures and remove concrete and other features from the main dwelling. You may also need to consider any new driveways, curbs and fencing that will be necessary.

Once approvals have been received for the civil engineering, you will need to get quotes from suitable contractors to carry out the works. There would be nothing stopping you from obtaining quotes before the approval as well. Quoting can be a difficult task; it is a good idea to get multiple quotes that accurately reflect the full requirements of the job in line with the council's requirements. Pricing can vary a lot, and the cheapest quotes may not necessarily be the best or the most accurate representation of the work. Talk with your contractors and get to the nitty gritty. The opposite can also apply and that is that overly expensive quotes are not necessarily the best, because they might include work that is not necessary.

Engage the most appropriate contractors, pay deposits, obtain work permits (where necessary) and, finally, dirt will get pushed, concrete laid, and the frame will start going up. For this process to run smoothly and efficiently the works need to be orchestrated. You never rely on the contractors to self-manage because the job may never get done. If you have the time, you can manage the process yourself but it's usually better to use a skilled project manager or project management consultancy to whip your contractors into shape. Appointment of a project manager needs to be made before work commences.

> **TIP:** Remember, it rains! The best schedules can be blown out due to weather conditions, so it is worth making allowances for this.

Fast-forward several months when works are complete and now you require a final survey plan to submit for 'plan sealing'. Primarily, this is another administrative process to ensure compliance and that the Ts & Cs have been satisfied. Once the council has inspected your completed development, and the boxes have been ticked, the survey plan is sealed. This means that everything is in order, and new lot numbers have been issued.

Once the plan is sealed, it will need to be registered with the Titles Office, and this completes the process.

## PUTTING IT INTO PRACTICE

So we've covered the theory, now let's look at some practical example development strategies.

Here are the assumptions we will make:

- All listings are under the appropriate zoning for the implied strategy

- Developments are 'fit for purpose' for the location and market expectations
- No consideration is given to the exit strategy for the purpose of simplicity.

## Strategy 1

An investor holds their principal place of residence and an additional investment property purchased ten years ago. The strategy is to manufacture equity and to pay for a small lot (670sqm) reconfiguration.

| | |
|---|---:|
| Original purchase price (2006) + costs | |
| (Interest only repayments on borrowings) | $300,000 |
| Development assessment | $50,000 |
| Dealing with the existing dwelling | |
| (reposition on the block plus renovations) | $190,000 |
| Total costs | $540,000 |
| Valuation | $850,000 |
| Improved position | $310,000 |

## Strategy 2

Investor 2 pursues a strategy focused on obtaining larger blocks (800sqm+), repositioning the existing dwelling, completing renovations and building a triplex at the back.

| | |
|---|---:|
| Acquisition, purchasing costs and DA | $1,000,000 |
| Dealing with the existing dwelling (repositioning | |
| on the block plus renovations) | $150,000 |
| Triplex construction | $900,000 |
| Total costs | $2,050,000 |
| Valuation | $2,400,000 |
| Improved position | $350,000 |

**WARNING:** It is becoming difficult to obtain good splitter blocks, particularly when you are running the feasibility and are focused on achieving a 20%+ margin, which is critical if you want to ensure longevity as a property developer.

## Strategy 3

Investor 3 looks for larger blocks to build '6-packs' and prefers to sell the properties at the finalisation of construction.

| | |
|---|---|
| Acquisition, purchasing costs and DA | $1,200,000 |
| Removing the existing dwelling | $25,000 |
| 6-pack construction | $2,000,000 |
| Total costs | $3,225,000 |
| Sales price | $3,900,000 |
| Improved position | $675,000 |

## Strategy 4

Investor 4 acquires a cleared and levelled site and develops a five-unit complex which is all on-sold.

| | |
|---|---|
| Acquisition | $580,000 |
| DA/BA/council/holding and misc. costs | $344,000 |
| Construction | $1,000,000 |
| Total costs | $1,924,000 |
| Sales price $500,000 (each) | $2,500,000 |
| After GST and selling costs | $2,296,000 |
| Profit | $372,000 |

Tax on $372,000 would be about $120,000, less if you have a good accountant, leaving an after-tax profit of $252,000. Now $120,000 is a fair chunk to be forking out in tax, but you can't get out of it. If you don't pay tax, you won't be able to get a loan to finance the next development because you haven't theoretically recorded a profit. Unfortunately, you have to pay tax. You can minimise it, but payment is required. We'll discuss this more in the following chapter.

To do a deal that stacks up like strategy 4, you would probably need a cash/equity position of between $450,000 to $500,000, and you won't need to kick all of that in at the start. Half would go up front for the purchase costs, DA and BA, and after that point construction finance would kick in, and you would progressively draw down funds. On these numbers, you would be looking at a return of more than 50% (after tax) and the project time would be 18 months (give or take) for completion. Making a 50% after-tax profit in 18 months is excellent, and you would be hard pushed to find a return like that on another asset class. This is not a standard-deal but there is money to be made in property development.

The numbers in the strategies above are rough but reasonably realistic. The examples are on the smaller side of potential developments, but they are indicative of creative and intelligent strategies everyday individuals are pursuing to generate wealth.

## DEVELOPMENT SUCCESS

Taking a project from conception to site acquisition, and through to design, approval, financing, construction, marketing and sales/leasing is a highly orchestrated process. Attitude, education and experience gained from prior successful and unsuccessful developments are the attributes of successful developers.

Anyone has the potential to succeed in development. The big boys complete larger-scale commercial and residential complexes, but most of the small- to medium-sized suburban developments are done by part-time developers/investors who maintain a full-time job. They are taking on development projects to fast-track their wealth.

If you're new to property development starting small is best. I originally started with a buy-and-hold strategy. My next experience was in renovating and flipping. Now I concentrate on smaller lot developments. I've taken gradual steps over time, which suits my lifestyle requirements and risk profile. I'm sure I'll change my approach again in the future with further experience.

The steps to development success are:

1. Prefeasibility – find the perfect site
2. Construction – within time and budget constraints
3. Managing risks
4. Deciding on a hold or exit strategy.

Let's look at each in turn.

## Prefeasibility

You've found a prospective site with the right zoning, infrastructure and lot size, in a perfect location. To secure it, it's highly likely that you have to pay at least fair market value – an offer of anything less and you'll be beaten by another developer who will snap it up. So now it is about the numbers and ensuring you can obtain at least a 20% margin. That way you can feel safe, knowing that there is enough 'fat' to cover any hiccups and missteps. Therefore, your preliminary feasibility needs to be accurate enough in the estimates across:

- Acquisition outlays
- Development approval costs
- Operational works
- Construction
- Sealing and title fees
- Selling costs.

You need to watch cash flow and budgets during the whole build phase through to completion.

The next step is construction.

## Construction

Even if your projects and numbers get larger and more complex, the construction steps will remain the same:

1. Site preparation:
   - Surveying and pegging to prepare for excavation and footings
   - Installing services – water, sewerage, draining, power, gas and phone
   - Levelling and filling of the site
   - Execution for the footings.

2. Base stage:
   - Stumps for the floor or slab will be completed in line with the soil conditions.

3. Frame stage:
   - Your development will start looking like a house now! Floor, walls, roof frame and windows go in.

4. Lock-up stage:
   - Brickworks or lighter weight material is applied to the eaves and doors are installed. The dwelling is now lockable.

5. Fixing stage:
   - Cabinets, benchtops, appliances, showers, baths, etc., are installed.

6. Completion:
   - Painting, fitting/fixtures installed, tiles and carpets are laid, landscaping and anything else stipulated in the contract is completed.

7. Variations:
   - Any adjustments made during the process need to be completed, as agreed in writing. The builder's margin of variation will be somewhere around the 20% mark.

8. Acceptance and completion:
   - Walk through with the builder and notify them of any defects before taking possession. Again this should be in writing and signed by both parties.

Depending on what has been agreed, the contract progress payments will be due at initial acceptance stage (in the form of a deposit) and then at the base, frame, lock-up and fixing stages and the balance at completion.

---

### Risks that need factoring into your feasibility scenarios

- Upward movements in interest rates that will increase your holding costs.
- Labour costs, reliability of the workers and the quality of their workmanship.
- Economic factors such as a downturn in the property market resulting in falling or slow growth that will put pressure on your holding costs.
- Disputes with builders and contractors.
- Changes to laws, zoning, planning, land use, environmental controls, stamp duty, land tax, etc.
- Over-capitalising – sinking cash into a property does not immediately equate to significant property value increases.
- Unexpected structural defects or building deficiencies incurring unaccounted for additional expenses.
- Weather – extended periods of rain will cause delays and could affect other building factors.

---

The best thing to do is take the risk-averse approach and allow for contingencies at each stage through your feasibility and forecasting.

Once compliance certificates are obtained, the next decision is to hold or to sell the asset. Realistically, this should be known well before this stage. Better yet, this should be known at the concept stage before the acquisition even.

Choosing to sell means that you will realise your returns now. The trade-off may be that you forfeit longer-term capital appreciation. As mentioned before, the challenge for property investors is managing exchange costs because they are huge. When you buy, an additional 5% (in some cases more) of the purchase price will be necessary to cover all the different purchasing costs. Therefore, when you sell and realise the profits to put into the next site, much of the return will go on the purchasing costs of the next one. A critical factor in determining success is careful thinking from the beginning to the end.

## JOINT VENTURING

Joint venturing is where two heads are better than one! Investors engage with partners for various reasons, including to pool finances, knowledge, skills, expertise and resources. By undertaking a joint venture (JV), you can accelerate your growth and reach your financial goals sooner. Partners can help you view things from a different perspective and create win-win outcomes. Conversely, JVs can be more time-consuming, and situations can change resulting in deviations from the original plan. The worst-case scenario is that you just get involved with completely the wrong partner!

New prospective partners realistically can come from all walks of life – through social or professional networking or the various property mentoring schemes that are available. The key is to identify someone who brings some different skills, yet shares the same property invest-ment strategy.

Success is far more likely if you find a partner you can trust, communicate with and maintain a relationship with. Make sure you have a Memorandum of Understanding (MOU) in place before finding the deal. You may be more commercially-minded than your JV partner(s) and able to organise and structure the finances and finalise the exit strategy. Your new partner may be strong on the project management and delivery. On paper, this looks like a formidable partnership.

Alternatively, you could be the landowner sitting on a gold mine yet lacking the means to realise its full potential – unless a partner can be found to share the burden of the planning and construction costs. The options the landowner might consider are an outright sale or to sell in stages at the development agreement and joint venture agreement stages.

Interested JV partners will be looking at the mutual profit in the deal and at who will contribute money, property or skill. The legal agreement should be carefully negotiated. Property lawyers will be able to draft a JV agreement that sets out the individual responsibilities and rights of the partners and defines the relationship as minimal essential requirements. Be careful not to structure your JV as a partnership which in most cases would be classed as an entity and, therefore, carries more liability and tax liabilities.

**WARNING:** You will need to consult an experienced property lawyer and/or accountant who is familiar with your individual circumstances before signing a joint venture agreement.

Objectives should be clear from the outset, and the agreement should cover:

- Details of the particular project
- Parties' names, responsibilities and specific contributions
- A budget (up-to-date financial records will be essential)

- How liability, profit or losses will be shared
- How expenses are paid
- In what circumstances the JV may be terminated
- A dispute resolution process and maybe the nomination of a third-party mediator.

Different circumstances will have different requirements and consultation with a solid accounting and tax professional and property lawyer will be essential.

### Joint venture structures

The legal structure established for a JV can be quite simple (in the names of the individuals), or more sophisticated (through an SMSF or family trust). For this reason alone, professional expertise is required for legal, accounting and finance product selection and structure.

A simple structure could be joint names:

**Figure 8: Joint venture in individual names**

Therefore, borrowing will be assessed on each individual's capacity to service the loan and set-up costs will be low. The downside to this structure is its ineffectiveness to provide asset protection and its constraints in tax planning.

A more complex structure could be establishing a property holding company (with an ABN and requirement to lodge a tax return). JV partners would own 'shares' in the company and company tax (at 30%) will have to be paid on profits. Funds will be distributed as franked dividends.

Figure 9: Joint venture in a company structure

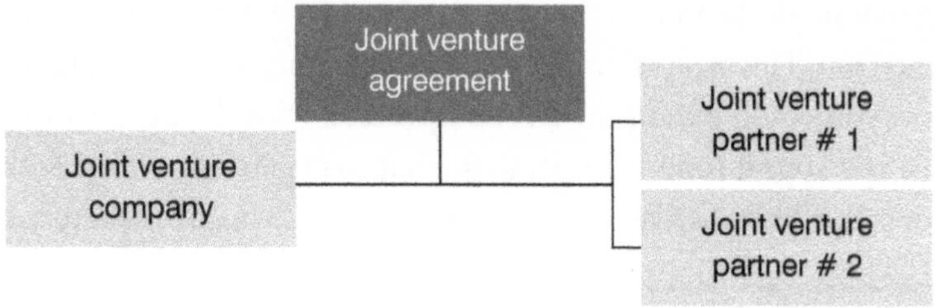

Alternatively, a unit trust could be established for the business activity. Then the unit trust will distribute the profits to the JV partners through their unit-holding. Again, the optimum structure should be discussed with your legal and accounting specialists.

The Buyers Guide has the right expertise and knowledge to assist when it comes to obtaining development funding. Keep in mind that if you are undertaking a large project, financing may need to be split over more than one lender. If this is your situation, you will also need to enlist the services of a good mortgage broker.

## LAND BANKING

Land banking is speculating that a large site will have more potential sometime in the future. Perhaps it can be subdivided into smaller parcels and sold off at a later date. Or maybe planning and zoning changes are due to take effect that will dramatically improve the land's development potential.

A common example of land banking is when residential developers purchase greenfield sites on the city outskirts. This provides a pipeline of stock for future development. Over time, the land will be rezoned, the necessary infrastructure will be in place and it will be possible to subdivide and sell off blocks individually.

Another example of land banking is purchasing a well-located dwelling that might be in the 'later' stages of its life, but which can still be rented out. This type of property will keep holding costs low, and over time, you could obtain the DA and proceed with the development. This is a sound long-term strategy that may allow you to ride the property cycle to strike at the opportune time to maximise returns.

### Potential land banking risks

- Zoning may not change, or it takes far longer than anticipated. Holding costs could be significant.
- The council may restrict the number of divided land titles.
- Population increases and demographics of the region may not meet expectations.
- Soil conditions could affect the feasibility of construction.
- There could also be restrictions on clearing vegetation.
- Scams! People have been caught out by developers who offer land that they don't own.

**TIP:** Research and due diligence are fundamental in obtaining the right product that appreciates in value based on the prospective changes in time.

## NO MONEY DOWN DEALS

'No money down' is a bit misleading because money does go down, it's just not your money. The aim in this situation is to use other people's money to do the deals. Now, if you're not bringing money to the agreement then you will need to bring something else to the table. You'll either have specific technical skills that can help advance the project or you can attract future buyers of the property to provide the necessary start-up capital.

Overall, this strategy involves a relatively high level of risk, due to the shorter timelines involved and the reliance on partners. You may seek distressed vendors with limited options – but these opportunities are scarce.

Depending on your risk profile and skills, there are a couple of methods to pursue if you want to do deals with little or no money down. These include:

- Buying a property off-the-plan before completion, hoping for the value to increase by the time it's completed and borrowing against the new value to fund the deposit. This strategy will only work when you are able to purchase the off-the-plan property at a great price in a growing market. The development will also need a long lead time for the magic of capital growth to take effect.
- Doing a joint venture where a partner can sponsor the upfront costs. In this arrangement, the partners can be equity or finance partners. Equity partners usually pay the deposit and cover buying costs and the finance partner obtains the loan and the proceeds are split.
- Finding a vendor to agree to an option. In this arrangement, you have the 'option' not the obligation to buy the property. You find a way to manufacture value and then on-sell the property to a new party for a profit. A small payment is made to the vendor which they keep if the 'option' is not exercised. There are a few vendors who agree to this proposal, particularly if they are in trouble or are having difficulty selling the property. It is a risky strategy and one in which your time and the vendor's time could perhaps be better spent elsewhere. But it is certainly possible to do.

These deals are done, but I'm a little suspicious of them due to their risky nature and the variables and timelines involved. The strategy with real merit is joint venturing, particularly if you lack finance but have a specialist skill, be it in finding the sites, or professional knowledge in the engineering, building or planning areas that would be advantageous to the financier. You put no money down but you will need to bring something to the deal. If you don't, why would a potential partner want to do business with you?

## NEW AND EMERGING INVESTMENT OPTIONS

The age of information is breaking down the barriers of entry to property investing, and new emerging technologies are helping to shift the pendulum.

Numerous quality online resources are providing information and research data, helping investors to make informed investment decisions. These create alternative entry points for wholesale and retail investors.

Crowdfunding is the latest option, with legislation pending that may transform the way the masses can invest in property. Technically, you should be able to purchase units in property directly from your mobile phone without even needing to visit the property directly. The 'armchair' investor currently exists, and is not far away from being at the fingertips of everyone. Just imagine if you could purchase a share in a blue chip property for less than $100.

Crowdfunding is a modern twist of what has existed for quite some time in the form of property trusts and syndicates. Usually, these investment vehicles are only offered to high-net-worth individuals who pool funds and pursue property assets such as commercial buildings, retail operations and industrial complexes. Since the GFC, these platforms have gone through a bit of a renaissance and increased in popularity. So, let's now explore these in some more detail.

## PROPERTY TRUSTS, SYNDICATES AND CROWDFUNDING

Property trusts or pooled funds have been around for a long time. Essentially they are professionally managed property funds, also called syndicates, that can provide an alternative method to invest in property. Investors buy 'units' in an investment property or properties, which are managed by the investment manager.

The funds 'pool' the money together to purchase commercial, retail or industrial property. So the sum of the parts in effect is greater than the whole. The power of the group can gain exposure to assets which may previously be out of reach, particularly on a large scale.

Syndicates have attracted some bad press for non-performance, particularly through the GFC. Their poor performance is usually linked to poor investment managers, rather than the funds themselves. This highlights the importance of completing your due diligence not only on the fund but also on those managing it.

Once you have invested in a syndicate, that initial capital is tied up until the property is sold and the proceeds are distributed among the pool of investors. The income generated is paid either monthly or quarterly.

The success of the fund or syndicate depends on the investment manager. They are responsible for due diligence and the 'picks' of the fund. After that, they manage the maintenance, administration, income collection and distribution.

Crowdfunding is the new emerging kid on the block, and it has the potential to transform the way we invest in property domestically.

Property trusts are usually reserved for wholesale or 'sophisticated' investors, on the basis that they are more prepared for the risks involved.

A sophisticated investor is someone who earns more than $250,000 per annum or holds $2.5m in net assets. Now this investor could be a good source for crowdfunding.

A commercial venture I'm personally involved in will bring a fresh approach to unit trust investing. Established in Brisbane, the focus is on creating investment funds up to $5m, targeting residential property investments. The platform will be positioned as a genuine alternative for real estate investing. Ultimately, it will be simple to use, transparent and allow you to access blue chip residential property in investment-grade locations. For further details and to register your interest, please visit **www.rentvesting.com.au**.

## CHAPTER SUMMARY

If you are investing in property to generate wealth, as you should be, and only read three items in this whole book, take note of the points below, as they are the fundamental steps to success:

1. Know your why and desired outcome(s)
2. Create a strategy by determining your:
   - Risk profile
   - Market factors
   - Timeframe
   - Growth and income preferences and needs.
3. Select the right strategy:
   - Passive
   - Active
   - Alternative or emerging.

Being crystal-clear on your objectives and getting these three steps right will set you in the right direction for success. Remember, you're the captain of the ship and you set the course through the choices you make throughout those three steps.

# [managing the money]

## A year from now you may wish
## you had started today

KAREN LAMBS

Wealthy individuals in Australia broadly fit into one of three categories. They are:

1. Born into wealth or inherit it
2. Earn very high incomes via some form of business or entrepreneurial activity
3. Make good financial decisions throughout their lifetimes.

The third of the three options is in stark contrast to the others. It also backs up the initial statistics from the ATO that prove that you can be an average wage-earner and make S.M.A.R.T investment decisions to secure your financial future.

Moving from where you currently stand to where you want to be requires clarification of the three steps to success that we have already outlined. Nailing this down leads to progress, and ultimately that's all you want to achieve. Month on month, year on year, if you're consistently ahead, you're getting somewhere, so hats off to you!

Making progress does require finance which is the next piece of the puzzle. For a lot of Australians, getting on top of their household accounts and debt(s) is the first part that will lead them to put the whole puzzle together.

## UNDERSTANDING DEBT

Debt is commonplace, so common in fact that almost everyone has it in one form or another. There is nothing to be embarrassed about by having it. It only becomes unmanageable when it is ignored and gets out of hand. Managing and maintaining your debt is easy to do when you understand what it is all about. By understanding why things are the way they are, you can find easy solutions to overcome your individual debt problems.

Debt is typically thought of as a dirty word because it is commonly synonymous with excess personal consumption. However, debt is also an excellent wealth creation tool. There is a distinction between the two and it is crucial to point out that not all debt is created equal! Debt would be so much easier to manage if it were. Understanding the subtle differences is critical because good debt and bad debt can often coexist.

What you want to achieve is to reduce and eliminate all non-tax deductible debt – in other words bad debt. After that, you need to structure the remaining debt – the good debt – in a fashion that maximises your ability to create wealth against a backdrop of numerous other financial matters relating to your individual circumstances.

As an example, you hypothetically come into an inheritance. You have $200,000 left to pay off on your home loan. You use the inheritance of $100,000 to buy shares. This may seem like the right thing to do, but it is not. The $100,000 should go to paying down your home loan, because this is non-tax deductible debt. Then you could borrow $100,000 to purchase shares, using equity in your property as security. This is because gearing (borrowing) to invest is a tax-deductible debt. It does not have to be shares you use borrowings to invest in, you could use the $100,000 to fund the purchase of your next investment property. The theory is the same.

### DEFINITION

**Tax-deductible debt.** If a debt is tax-deductible you can usually claim a tax deduction for any expenses incurred in holding the asset you have borrowed money to invest in. With shares, you may be able to claim brokerage charges and interest on your loan. With property you can usually claim interest on your investment loan and maintenance and property management costs.

**Non tax-deductible debt.** The most common type of non tax-deductible debt is a home loan. There are no allowable deductions you can claim when you borrow to purchase your principal place of residence.

---

### Five common debt management mistakes

1. Individuals or a couple having several different debts, e.g. credit cards, a car loan, personal loan and home loan, and not combining the debt or using the equity in their home to repay the debts with higher interest rates.

2. Maintaining a 100% offset account with a home loan and not maximising its full potential. Choosing a home loan product with all the bells and whistles and not using the product features is a waste. And it won't create the best value for money.

3. Incorrect structures wrapped around the investments. It is important to understand the differences between good and bad debt as one is tax-deductible and the other isn't.

4. Couples that purchase investment property together and hold it in joint names at a 50/50 ownership ratio when one partner earns significantly less than the other. It would generally be more advantageous to have the property title in the name of the higher wage earner for tax purposes, or increase the ownership ratio to 80:20 in favour of the high income earner. If there are concerns regarding ownership because of a future potential break up, don't worry because the Family Court has a funny way of working this kind of stuff out. Family Law will usually override ownership title. However, if there are doubts about the longevity of a relationship to begin with you should probably question if purchasing property or other assets for that matter together is a wise decision.

5. Retaining a former principal place of residence as a rental. Putting sentimental attachment aside, this isn't usually the best option. Home-owners generally work quite diligently to pay off their family home, so there isn't a lot to claim against for tax purposes, when then rent it out. Higher maintenance costs may also be incurred if it is an older property, therefore they may not be able to maximise depreciation allowances. If you are looking at investment property for wealth creation, as you should be, then it makes more sense to use the money

to pay down personal debt and then redraw on equity to purchase investments. You want to keep your personal debt low and investment debt high. Also this ensures you achieve the holy grail of investing, which is making investment decisions with your head and not your heart.

## Debt reduction

If you currently have some bad debts, try these immediate debt-reducing steps:

- Consolidate all personal debts at the lowest interest rate you can find, and use a line of credit or a redraw facility with a 100% offset account attached to this loan account. Maintain the pre-consolidation repayments – the same applies if there are any future interest rate cuts. Direct all income and savings into your offset account or line of credit. Any windfalls such as work bonuses or tax returns should be added too.
- Use a 55-day interest-free credit card to keep your loan account balance low, offsetting interest for longer. Pay the credit card off before interest is charged, but unless you are entitled to discounts for early payment, pay all of your bills at the 11th hour. You want to maximise the opportunity to hold your cash for as long as possible offsetting the existing interest in your loan account. The compounding effect of the savings can shave thousands of dollars and years off your mortgage.
- With all funds (income, savings, bonuses, money put aside for monthly expenses) accumulating in your offset account, a budget can help you keep track of spending.
- Consider other investments to get ahead – reducing debt requires income, to earn more you can trade more hours for

more income or acquire income-producing assets, this is where equity plays a vital role.

- Separate yourself from your investments. For this to work you need to know your available cash flow, establish an investment plan and contribute regularly to savings or repayments. Seek advice and ensure the right structures are in place, along with correct cash flow calculations.

**TIP:** Seeking additional professional guidance will help your wealth creation plans and hopefully switch them to auto-pilot.

## DEBT STRUCTURING

As previously stated, debt structuring requires careful consideration against the backdrop of all other financial matters relating to your individual circumstances. Structuring debt as effectively as possible to meet your needs can be a powerful wealth creation strategy that will allow for the further acquisition of income-producing assets that grow in value over time. Effective debt structuring will serve four purposes when you are creating wealth:

1. Reduce tax payable each financial year
2. Reduce fees on complex lending facilities
3. Reduce interest payable on debt
4. Improve cash flow.

However, it must be noted that there is no one-size-fits-all approach. Individual circumstances, needs, wants, goals, risk profiles and strategy can differ greatly.

**TIP:** If you would like a free personal assessment on your current debt structures, then reach out to **www.thebuyersguide.com.au**.

# FINANCIAL STRATEGIES

Having worked our way through debt, the next piece of the puzzle is financial strategy. Within our banking, superannuation, investment and taxation systems there are numerous methods people use to improve their financial positions. Let's look now at the strategies most commonly used for creating wealth through property investing.

## Strategy #1 – negative gearing

As we mentioned previously, negative gearing is a favoured property investing strategy because of the ability to 'gear up' or leverage into property at higher loan-to-value ratios (LVRs) without having to sell the investment if the market heads south. This is a distinct advantage over shares, as you will not be faced with a margin call as long as repayments are met.

Negative gearing doesn't always mean that you have to suffer a real income loss. Because of tax add-backs, like depreciation, it is possible to claim all the tax deductions associated with negative gearing but maintain a positive cash flow. For many investors, their higher-yielding investments will start paying for themselves from day one, even though borrowings can be 100% of the purchase price.

Tax benefits can be significant, making an investment cash flow positive, even for investors with more moderate incomes.

### Advantages of negative gearing
1. Higher gearing ratios are achieved with property than shares
2. Higher salaries can equate to higher deductions
3. Ownership and lending structures can have a large effect on the tax consequences

4. If you use net yield figures to assess affordability on new properties, when you crunch the numbers the results tend to be higher due to larger depreciation allowances
5. Tax variations on your personal income can improve your cash flow
6. It gives you a good chance of growth, growth, growth – which is where wealth is made.

## Strategy #2 – superannuation

Why do Australians love their superannuation? Because it's the closest thing to an offshore tax haven! Significant tax advantages are available through super, and we all love to pay less tax. The maximum tax you pay when you put money into a super fund is 15% of your gross income, not your net income. This compares with the highest rate of tax of 49% you would pay on the same earnings if you were in the highest marginal tax bracket.

If you have a self-managed super fund (SMSF), you can control the timing of this tax and reduce it further with negative gearing or by claiming expenses such as personal insurance premiums. This means you can reduce tax payable to even less than 15%.

Capital gains tax (CGT) payable by a superannuation fund is 15% of net profits, instead of 49% if you sell an asset held outside of super within 12 months of acquisition. After 12 months, the CGT rate reduces to a maximum of 24.5% outside of super and only 10% within super. If you sell the asset after retirement, and it is held in your SMSF, you won't pay anything!

Self managed super gives you greater control but additional responsibilities come with it. There are administrative tasks that take time to manage and it is costly to set up a fund initially. If you are considering purchasing property with an SMSF, get professional advice when you are establishing the fund and to advise on ongoing management. Penalties for non-compliance can be very expensive which makes the small associated management fees well worthwhile.

## Advantages of superannuation

1. Super can't be accessed until you retire. You need to realise it will be for the long term. The big advantage of this is a beautiful little thing called compounding (see next section)!
2. Healthy tax savings are achieved through super.
3. SMSFs are advantageous because they give you control, allow you to purchase property through gearing and there are some estate planning benefits too.

## Strategy #3 – debt separation

We have discussed good and bad debt in some detail, and now I tell you how to make your debt situation as efficient as possible by debt separation. Debt separation is a method of structuring investments in a way that transfers your bad debt to good debt as efficiently as possible.

Most people are paid directly into their savings account. Then they move that income to their home loan, use it to pay off credit cards, personal loans, and for living expenses, holidays and emergencies. Money in your savings account will pay an interest rate of less than 1% (at time of writing). If it's a high-interest saver account or a term deposit, at the moment, it will probably pay less than 3% (at best).

Now, you may also have a home mortgage with $300,000 owing, and you're paying an interest rate of 5%. It is important to note that when you borrow money from the bank, you are charged interest at 5% and when they borrow money from you (the money in that savings account), the bank pays you less than 1%!

To take advantage of debt separation, you first need to establish a 100% offset facility attached to your home loan. If you have already done this then start using it straightaway. A line of credit facility can also be used, (both products are very similar), but most people find offset accounts easier to manage.

The next step is to have all your income paid directly into the offset account. That money will now offset the balance owing on your home loan. Therefore, it will reduce the interest that would be payable. Each dollar you have in the offset account saves you interest at 5%. You are also not paying tax on interest earned in a savings account.

Now the focus can shift to part two of the strategy. In this scenario, assume you have a mortgage of $300,000 on a property valued at $550,000. Most lenders will lend up to 80% of the property value without incurring lender's mortgage insurance (LMI). So, 80% of $550,000 is $440,000. If you owe $300,000 that means you have $140,000 of equity available. So you can keep $40,000 in the offset account as a buffer (a rainy day fund) and move the remaining $100,000 into a separate lending facility. You can now use that $100,000 as a deposit to purchase your next investment property. Once that money is spent it becomes tax-deductible and the rental income received is paid into the 100% offset facility, reducing non-deductible debt faster. Once more equity is built up, the next step is to repeat!

### DEFINITION

**Lender's mortgage insurance (LMI).** Some lenders will lend you more than 80% of the value of a property, but if they do you will be charged LMI. This insurance covers the lender (not you!) in the event that you can no longer service your loan and the lender has to foreclose on the loan and sell your property at a loss to recoup the loan money. LMI is a once-off payment made when you take out the loan and it can be anything from 0.5% to several percentage points of the entire loan amount. The variance is based on the loan amount and applicable loan-to-value ratio.

Over time, this strategy will save you thousands of dollars in interest, cut years off your mortgage and at the same time build an investment nest-egg.

## Modern investment fundamentals

OK, there are many, but here are a few things that hold true no matter how modern the times:

1. Investors with time and patience on their side, and the discipline to stay the course, are well rewarded in the long run.
2. Diversification and risk management strategies that align with your risk profile will help you sleep better at night.
3. Yield and growth are equally as important. Yield should cover your costs as best as possible and then capital growth should be the aim and the 'cream' on top.
4. Don't speculate! The age-old saying still applies, "If it sounds too good to be true, it probably is…"

## Strategy #4 – risk management

We won't cover too much detail here because we explore risk management in Chapter 4. However, risk is everywhere, and we do risky things every day and think nothing of it. We almost all drive daily, it's probably one of the most dangerous things we do – a white line is the only thing that separates us from a potential accident. However, we have all built up expertise to prevent incidents. Our vehicles are better protected and, in turn, we protect those vehicles.

You need to apply the same risk mitigation strategies in your property investing. You want to build up your expertise and minimise expensive capital outlays should an 'incident' occur.

Here are some key points to remember about risk management:

1. Insurance is the foundation of any wealth creation plan. The premiums should be viewed as an investment cost.
2. Insurance premiums can generally be paid through your superannuation fund.
3. Insurance can be used effectively for estate planning purposes.

## THE MAGIC OF COMPOUNDING

Before we go further, I need to remind you of the power of compounding to explain why property is a long-term investment. Compounding is the secret weapon, it's like a magic wand. Now let's wave that magical wand and create two options.

1. Accept $1m right now: or
2. Accept 1¢ that doubles every day for 30 days.

Which one would you take? You would take the $1m hands down! A great result – $1m cash – how good is that? Well, not as good as the value of a doubling cent! Let's look at that value in 30 days in time.

It is not until day 27 that it starts to go gangbusters! Much the same as property, the longer you hold it, the more valuable it will be, giving you all the more reason to stay the course with your investment. The property is ten times more likely to double in value over ten years. Long-term is the best term.

## Table 5: Compounding effect of doubling a 1¢ every day for 30 days

| Day 1 2¢ | Day 2 4¢ | Day 3 8¢ | Day 4 16¢ | Day 5 32¢ |
|---|---|---|---|---|
| Day 6 64c¢ | Day 7 $1.28 | Day 8 $2.56 | Day 9 $5.12 | Day 10 $10.14 |
| Day 11 $20.28 | Day 12 $40.56 | Day 13 $81.12 | Day 14 $162.24 | Day 15 $324.48 |
| Day 16 $648.96 | Day 17 $1,297.92 | Day 18 $2,595.84 | Day 19 $5,191.68 | Day 20 $10,383.36 |
| Day 21 $20,766.72 | Day 22 $41,533.44 | Day 23 $83,066.88 | Day 24 $166,133.76 | Day 25 $332,267.52 |
| Day 26 $664,535.04 | Day 27 $1,329,070.08 | Day 28 $2,658,140.16 | Day 29 $5,316,280.32 | Day 30 $10,632,560.64 |

## CHOOSING THE RIGHT FINANCING STRATEGY FOR YOU

It is important that an investment strategy is specific to each individual investor, and it is impossible to compare outcomes for every different investor. In most cases, property is a long-term investment unless you possess particular expertise or develop knowledge in renovation and flipping or property development. However, there are common considerations in whatever financial strategy you choose.

The first is effective financing:

- Work out how much you are going to spend (capital outlay including costs)
- How much will you need to borrow?
- How are you best going to hold the assets to maximise income and tax effectiveness?

Every investor's answers will be different because every scenario will be slightly different. It's important to note that while tax efficiency is key, you don't want to get the point where you are potentially flirting with tax avoidance. It's never a wise move, as one, it's illegal, two, penalties are severe, and lastly, you do need to produce a profit, in order to continue securing new finance.

The second consideration is the return on your money – yield and/or growth. Many factors can influence the yield and long-term capital growth a property can deliver – location, demographics, comparable sales, infrastructure, employment prospects, the dwelling itself, etc. Remember, long-term growth is far more efficient in producing wealth than yield. Table 6, below gives a great example of this.

### Table 6: Why is growth important?

| Growth in value of a $500,000 property over 20 years | | | |
|---|---|---|---|
| | Yield 7% | Growth 4% | Yield 4% | Growth 7% |
| 1 | $35,000 | $20,000 | $20,000 | $535,000 |
| 5 | $35,000 | $630,892 | $20,000 | $701,274 |
| 10 | $35,000 | $767,574 | $20,000 | $983,571 |

As you can see, lower yield and higher growth offers superior returns. Astute investors focus on growth.

The problem with this scenario is that you must satisfy the cash flow requirements to service the loan repayments. If you are on a low to medium income and cannot support periods of vacancy, or cover expenses associated with holding the property, or interest rate rises, then you may need to pursue an income strategy.

You must satisfy the cash flow requirements, or else you will find yourself struggling to make ends meet. You will be trapped in a job you may not even like because you've invested yourself into a corner. Worse still is having to sell your property before recouping your costs.

Conversely, high-income earners can cover expenses and claim any associated tax depreciation.

Even though growth may produce a better result over a 20-year period, it may be better for some investors to have at least one strong yielding property which will help cover the commitments of other growth properties in their portfolio.

As we've established already, ideally, you will have a combination of both growth and high-yielding properties held in appropriate structures. That way you will be able to move income between the negative and positively geared property to satisfy cash flow and taxation requirements.

## Common mistakes that investors make

1. Not making cash flow projections on expected revenues. Cash flow is the lifeblood of any business. When you're making cash flow projections be sure to use the net yield figures.
2. Concentrating solely on yield and assuming growth will just happen. Yield is important, undoubtedly, but growth is equally if not more important. Plus, growth isn't guaranteed, and you need to ensure before committing to the property that it has the right fundamentals to achieve growth.
3. Investing emotionally and losing focus on the numbers. Buying the little cute old house in the belief others will share the same love for it doesn't make a good investment.
4. Buying a property that you would love to live in yourself. It could also be a great investment but the fringe benefits will detract from the overall performance. It is best to acquire boring, low maintenance, money-making property. Focus on numbers and you'll have all the money you'll need in the long term to buy your dream beachfront home!

5. Renting out the former family home because, as we explained earlier, the tax-deductible component will quite likely be small. And the new non tax-deductible debt will be higher – this is the wrong way around. It is best to sell the old home, reduce the non-deductible debt and borrow the maximum amount for the new investment property.
6. Using the incorrect structure to wrap around your investment debt.
7. Concentrating purely on the purchase price. Yes, the price is of immense importance, and you make your money when you buy. But saving $20,000 on a low-growth investment and paying market value on a high-growth investment over the long term is wiser. You may save $20,000 initially but over the long term the saving will be insignificant.

## THE IMPORTANCE OF INCOME

Income is the lifeblood of a successful investment strategy and lack of income is the biggest factor preventing individuals from not creating a substantial property portfolio. There are many reasons for poor income returns, but two common ones are bad property selection and using the wrong financial structure.

For most investors, the largest source of income will come from their employment or the wage drawn from their business or entrepreneurial ventures. There could be rental revenue from existing investment properties or dividends distributed from a share portfolio too.

Few of us can afford to purchase property outright, and as we've previously outlined, when debt is correctly used, it is a tool for wealth creation. Therefore, since we need to borrow money to purchase property, we require income to service the loan. Serviceability is becoming increasingly important in the highly regulated realm of the Australian banking sector.

Some things that banks look for before they agree to lend you money are:

1. Will you be putting some of your own money into financing the deal? If so, make sure you have enough to cover the shortfall.
2. What equity or security do you have? Banks want concrete assets as collateral, not boats and furniture. When crunching your numbers reduce your assets' values by 20% because that's what the banks will do in their valuation.

If you are undertaking a development, banks will look for:

1. Serviceability to make repayments – income!
2. Your ultimate plan. Are you selling up once the project is complete or looking to achieve pre-sales?
3. Security for the loan.
4. Industry experience – what experience do you have if things go horribly wrong?

An important question to ask yourself is: "Is my starting point realistic?"

One thing to remember is that income is expressed as a cash flow, and yield is expressed as a ratio.

They are different concepts and they should not be confused. Decisions should be made on total rates of return after costs, not just on income alone.

The Australian Prudential Regulation Authority (APRA) has been pulling some strings behind the scenes, and that has meant lenders have been tightening lending policies in 2015-16 for investors. One thing they are doing is keeping a very close eye on serviceability. Lenders are increasingly looking for further documentation to support serviceability claims, and they have moved away from applying minimum rates for expenditure (30% to 35%). It is also important to remember in your calculations that lenders will assess rental income at 80% per annum (i.e. allowing for periods of vacancy).

When crunching your numbers, it is crucial to get your figures right – especially when planning your cash flow projections. Some points to remember are:

1. Consider the tax effects of who owns the property (if purchasing with a life partner), as tax deductions will be more generous for the higher income earner.
2. When calculating net yield, allow for expenses such as body corporate fees, insurances, property management fees, maintenance costs, council rates, water costs and vacancy rates. Also, run a second set of numbers to allow for upward fluctuations in interest rates.
3. Repairs and maintenance on newer buildings are usually lower than on older properties. Newer property often has lower vacancy rates. When you take depreciation into account too, newer property can achieve higher yields making it more cost-effective for investors on modest incomes.

Taking out income protection insurance is critical, and it will improve your serviceability profile (more about insurance in Chapter 4). Your biggest asset is you and your ability to produce income. Revenue generated from working will influence a lender's willingness to lend you money.

## OWNERSHIP STRUCTURES

It is far better to take the time at the beginning of your investment journey to decide what structure is going to work best for you. Fundamentally, the long-term implications around taxation and associated holding and offloading costs can make all the difference in the right structure. So take the time to review your options and speak with several different specialists to help you decide what structure will be best for you. Selecting the right structure will have long-term benefits. Conversely, getting it wrong can be quite problematic.

Remember, there is no one 'right' structure for all investors. The structure you choose will suit your individual circumstances. You will need to consider these different questions:

- How will income be distributed? Who will receive it? When will they receive it? How will they receive it, both now and in the future?
- What considerations should be given to your family regarding ownership and income, both now and in the future?
- How flexible does this structure need to be?
- What will be the most tax-effective structure?
- What arrangements will be made relating to estate planning?
- Will the assets be disposed of at some point in the future? Or will they be passed on?

These are all important questions to ask to determine the correct way forward.

We've talked a bit about structures already but now let's consider in more detail the five basic structures open to property investors:

1. Individual/sole trader
2. Partnership

3. Company
4. Trust
5. Self managed superannuation fund (SMSF).

Each of these structures has different tax implications, and each comes with a different set of risks.

## Individuals

Investing in your own name as an individual is the most common form of ownership structure. It has a lot going for it – it's simple and cheap!

Another favourite reason is that you can take advantage of negative gearing which can reduce your personal tax liability. This is not possible if the property is held in a trust structure.

The main disadvantage of investing as individuals is that you are taxed at your personal tax rate. You will be eligible for the 50% CGT discount as we noted earlier, but you could be taxed as highly as at 49% on 50% of any net capital gains if you are a high income earner. What also works against this structure is that you cannot re-distribute income in the same way that you can if you invest in a trust structure.

Another big drawback to this structure is that it is weak when it comes to asset protection. If you find yourself in an unfortunate circumstance and get sued or run into financial difficulty, there will be no asset protection.

As we mentioned earlier, a big mistake some people make is holding the property in joint names when one of the individuals earns significantly more than the other.

## Figure 10: Investing as an individual

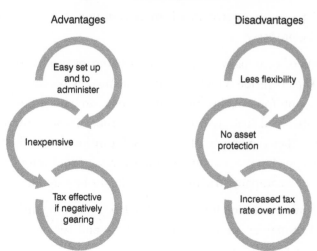

Partnerships

Again, it is the simplicity and cost-effectiveness of investing through partnerships that are the drawcards. A partnership, as opposed to holding in joint names, is a separate entity for tax purposes and requires its own tax file number and tax return. The partnership doesn't pay tax directly, but the individuals pay tax on income distributed by the partnership. The number of partners and the percentage ownership of each partner dictates how the income is distributed.

Risk protection again is weak through a partnership. Any of the partners' assets can become subject to a creditor's claim, and the other partners will also become liable. This is potentially a big risk in that one partner could become liable for all the partnership debts.

## Company

The use of a company structure is more common in business than for holding property.

The benefit of a company structure is tax – company profits are taxed at 30%. The downside is that companies are not eligible for the 50% CGT discount. You can't just rip funds out of a company for personal use, profits are distributed through dividends. Losses cannot be distributed, they can only be offset against future income, so they can become trapped in the company. If you're investing for the long term in property, a company structure may not be the best option.

There is some protection for the shareholders if the company fails or is sued. Companies are expensive to set up and separate sets of accounts are required at tax time.

The protection and reduced tax rate are lovely cherries, and if used appropriately in an overall strategy an investor may benefit from a company structure.

## Trusts

A trust is a legal relationship between the trustee who holds the asset for the benefit of the trust's beneficiaries. The trustee of a discretionary or family trust has the power to decide which of the beneficiaries will benefit from the trust. Trust structures provide the most flexibility and have some other bells and whistles:

1.  They are tax effective on the basis that income and capital can be distributed through to the beneficiaries who pay tax at lower rates. Overall, the tax paid by the family group can be reduced by paying different levels of income to various beneficiaries.
2.  Assets in the discretionary trust are separate from the assets of beneficiaries, offering some protection from lenders if a

beneficiary faces legal action or bankruptcy. No one single person owns any assets so creditors pursuing an individual cannot access a trust's property.

3. Losses can be carried forward to offset future gains. A discretionary trust has the entitlement to the 50% CGT discount when an asset is disposed of after it has been held for more than 12 months.

Trusts are popular because of their tax efficiency and the flexibility they offer in income distribution to the beneficiaries, whoever they may be. Although, the lifespan of a trust can be extensive, it is not 'evergreen'. A trust reaching the end of its term is usually known as the 'vesting period.'

Trusts will work best for a couple or a family that holds, or is building, a portfolio of revenue-generating assets with anticipated capital gains. If one of the beneficiaries pays tax at a lower tax rate, the trust will work well. Trusts are helpful in estate planning, particularly if the intention is to pass the asset ownership down to the next generation.

## Unit trusts

Unit and hybrid trusts are variations on the trust structure. Unit trusts provide a suitable structure for unrelated parties doing business with one another. Each investor has a predetermined entitlement depending on the units held. Those entitlements can be income or capital, or both. People use unit trusts to hold property, and the unitholder is the family trust.

Hybrid trusts are the birth child of discretionary trusts and unit trusts because they've been mixed together to create one entity. They can be used to gear into the property where an individual borrows to purchase units in the trust. Then when the property is no longer geared, the trust can re-buy the units, borrowing money to do so.

## Self managed superannuation funds (SMSFs)

An SMSF is a type of trust structure that has been all the rage recently. There has been a strong take up by consumers keen to take control of how their super is invested. If a husband and wife set up an SMSF, they become the trustees and members of the fund, and they are then responsible for the fund's operation.

Realistically, as a minimum, you'll need $200,000+ to set up an SMSF, and you need a sound investment strategy outlining what it is that you plan to do with money you accumulate in the SMSF. Set-up costs will be upwards of $2,000 and annual fees total around $1,500. The government is starting to look very carefully at SMSFs, so if you're up to anything naughty and get caught, you can expect hefty fines to follow.

As we previously outlined, the biggest attraction of SMSFs is the 15% tax rate they pay on income and capital gains. However, super is a long-term game because the funds are preserved until retirement. As the legislation currently stands, all revenue and capital gains generally become tax-free once you reach 60 years of age and are retired.

If you're focused on retirement planning as opposed to debt reduction and have a decent super balance and the ability to administer the fund according to appropriate regulations, then this structure could be well worth considering.

**WARNING:** I am by no means a legal, accounting or taxation expert, so it is of the utmost importance to obtain suitable professional advice relevant to your own individual circumstances before making investment decisions. Managing your own super is time-consuming, the compliance is onerous and you carry all the risk. For these reasons it is not always a suitable strategy for everyone.

## Investment structure summary

Figure 11 overleaf summarises ownership structures starting at the low end of establishment costs and detailing potential user benefits and drawbacks.

## Making changes and the costs involved

If you've always just done your own thing and built a nice little property portfolio that you anticipate growing further in the long term, well done! As you become more involved and knowledgeable, you may decide that you want to change structures. Before you do so, perhaps apply the handbrake and consider the costs involved because they can be substantial.

First, when you modify the ownership of property, you need to lodge a stamped Transfer of Land with the Titles Office. That stamp will come from the State Revenue Office, therefore, triggering a 'stamp duty event' levied on the current property's value. This expense will likely be in the tens of thousands of dollars.

Second, the transfer will also trigger a 'capital gains event' unless it is your principal place of residence. The CGT will be charged on the difference between the cost base of the asset and its market value when transferred. If the property is held for an extended period, it is likely the value will have increased significantly, meaning that the CGT alone could be enough to put you off pursuing the ownership change.

Last, transfers could also mean additional loan charges, legal, accounting, valuation and other miscellaneous costs. These will be small compared to the CGT and stamp duty, but again they need to be accounted for to give an accurate depiction of the overall cost.

## Figure 11: Investment structure summary

### Lower cost

**Individual**

- No asset protection from outside claims
- Taxed at the investor's marginal tax rate (can be as high as 49%)
- Poor flexibility
- Losses can be distributed

**Partnership**

- No asset protection from outside claims
- Taxed at the investor's marginal tax rate (can be as high as 49%)
- Poor flexibility
- Losses can be distributed

### Medium cost

**Company**

- Asset protected from outside risks if owned by a discretionary trust
- Taxed at 30%
- Fair amount of flexibility
- Losses cannot be distributed

**Unit Trust**

- Asset protected from outside risks if owned by a discretionary trust
- Taxed at the top marginal rate or 30% if unit holder is a company
- Good amount of flexibility
- Losses cannot be distributed

### High cost

**Discretionary Trust**

- Assets are protected from outside risk
- Taxed at the top marginal rate or 30% if the beneficiary is a company
- Very good level of flexibility
- Losses cannot be distributed

**Superannuation Fund**

- Assets are protected from outside risk
- Taxed at 15% if it is a complying fund
- Flexibility is fairly poor
- Losses cannot be distributed

When speaking with your professional advisers have them develop scenarios to help build a picture of the costs involved.

As you can see, these costs can be substantial so you will need to carefully assess and weigh up the long-term benefits of changing ownership structures. In the end, you may find that the juice won't be worth the squeeze!

## TAXATION OF STRUCTURES

When it comes to tax matters, get good advice and get it early. The tax affairs of most property investors will be relatively straightforward: allowable deductions will be offset against income. However, when you start tackling something out of the ordinary, tax issues can get significantly more complex.

As a hypothetical example, if you wanted to sell off several developments in a completed project, but retain a few units for yourself to produce a rental income, and hold them in a family trust, then you will need good professional advice. From a taxation perspective, there are numerous moving parts in this scenario, so you need to engage with a strong accountant who understands property and is ideally investing and developing themselves.

Often companies are used as a development vehicle, and trusts are used to hold the assets. Unlike companies, trusts may be eligible for the 50% CGT discount on profits from the asset's sale. If a company and trust that you control enters into a JV to develop the property, the costs can be shared proportionately and you can split the asset on completion. Complex? Yes, that's why you need advice and need it early.

Getting your tax structures right from the start is key. With the proper planning, you could develop at cost, earn rent in the meantime, and pay half the tax on eventual disposal.

The following are aspects of taxation that property investors need to be familiar with.

## The goods and services tax (GST)

Residential property investors don't need to concern themselves with GST but as soon as you get involved in developing property or investing in commercial property GST will be involved.

## Capital gains tax (CGT)

Capital gains tax (CGT) is paid when you realise those gains – when you sell property that is not your principal place of residence. It is calculated at an individual's tax rate if you have invested in your own name and/or that of your life partner. It can be a tough pill to swallow after years of holding, as the tax can be substantial. But a significant tax bill also means a significant profit has been made, so well done!

CGT applies to all assets, not just property, including managed funds and shares. Your personal residence is exempt from CGT and if you have purchased your property on or before 20th September 1985, that asset will also be exempt.

As noted earlier, your primary residence is exempt from CGT. However, you cannot own two properties and live alternately between the properties to avoid paying CGT! If you rent out a property straight away, the ATO will deem its acquisition was for investment purposes. If you hold it for more than 12 months, and it is considered to be subject to CGT, you will be entitled to claim the 50% CGT discount. Also, under the 'six-year rule' if you move out of your primary residence, rent it out and sell the property within six years, you may still be exempt from CGT, as long as another new principal place of residence is not claimed. Each situation varies so seek professional tax advice before making decisions. Remember, get advice and get it early.

MANAGING THE MONEY

## Allowable deductions

If you borrow to buy an investment property, the interest on your loan and other costs (see below) are deducted from the rental income, and if a loss is produced then this may be deducted from your other assessable income which lowers your overall taxable income. Now, if cash flow is critical, you don't need to wait a year to lodge your tax return. Your accountant can complete an Income Tax Withholding Variation form that takes your losses into account, and your regular pay can be adjusted so you get a proportion of the tax return each pay cycle. This can significantly help your cash flow and make interest repayments easier.

Tax deductions are wide-ranging as are the running, maintenance and management costs of your investments. Some of the deductions you can claim are:

1. Property management fees
2. Council and water rates
3. Advertising costs when you're looking to attract tenants
4. Insurance
5. Interest on investment loans
6. Travel expenses to the property (within reason)
7. Depreciation.

You will need to keep all receipts, documents and bank statements as part of your record-keeping, along with an accurate depreciation schedule and capital works sheet. A quantity surveyor can save you significant sum of money in the long run by putting together a depreciation schedule, outlining how much you can claim each year. Depreciation can save you thousands of dollars over the life of your investment. The tax office refers to depreciation as 'non-cash deductions' meaning that you haven't physically paid out cash to claim the deduction. It's a deduction for the wear and tear of the

95

property. The building itself, as well as the plant and equipment, will become worn out over time and need replacing. It doesn't matter who pays for them originally, you as the current owner can continue to claim deductions as they depreciate.

Once you have a depreciation schedule prepared by a quantity surveyor, you hand it over to your accountant and that's pretty much all you have to do.

Whether you own the property in your own name, through a trust or SMSF, always seek financial advice relating to your tax structures, allowable deductions and minimisation strategies.

## LOAN AND FINANCE STRUCTURING

The secret weapon for any property investor is leverage. Good debt can become a powerful tool for wealth generation. When structured appropriately, the value of growth assets, like property, can increase at a higher rate compared to the actual cost of borrowing. Creating equity becomes a lot more efficient than paying the debt with surplus funds. Plus, investment debt becomes tax-deductible, adding another cherry to the equation.

Using good debt and your borrowing power will determine your ability to succeed as an astute property investor. If you establish your portfolio in the right way, from the outset, it becomes very easy to build wealth. You need to consider your investment plan and think two or three loans ahead.

People often make the mistake of sticking with one lender and cross-securitising their properties. Or they focus solely on the short-term interest rate offered when they select a loan, forgetting that the right structure, or a line of credit, can offer substantial interest savings over the life of the loan.

**DEFINITION**

**Cross-securitisation.** Cross-securitisation (also referred to as cross-collateralisation) describes the situation where a loan is secured by more than one property. A common example is where an investor has equity in their own home and uses this as security to purchase an investment property.

Loan structuring is very individualistic as many variables influence the outcomes. Plus, there are dozens of lenders and hundreds of different products available, each with their individual characteristics.

---

### Factors that influence a loan structure

- The five Cs of – credit, character, capital, collateral and capacity
- Time frames – short or long term
- Active or passive investment options
- Risk tolerance
- Need and desire to pay down debt
- Flexibility.

---

Not only should you consider what is best for you now, but also how your decisions will impact you in the future. Having a clear plan for your property investment will guide the decisions you make around finance and structure, and influence the debt facilities you choose. As I've said before, the right structure could save you a fortune and allow you to more efficiently build a profitable portfolio. The intention over the next few pages is to help you do just that.

Setting your loan structure correctly (i.e. in line with your investment strategy) will create half a dozen positive outcomes:

1. **Tax efficiencies** – optimising your tax position will help improve cash flow and cash flow is the lifeblood for any growing property portfolio. A common problem faced is the inefficient split of deductible and non-deductible debt. Larger loans should be used to finance tax-deductible debt and interest costs can be offset against your income. If the more substantial debt is associated with your home loan this is not possible. Don't make the mistake of your home loan being too large a proportion of your total debt.

2. **Flexibility** to be opportunistic! Your loan structuring should allow you to access money quickly to take advantage of an opportunity when it arises, or refinance if a lender comes out with a cracking new rate. Flexibility is essential because you will want and need to make changes from time to time.

3. **Better risk management** to cover scenarios that may impede your ability to maintain repayments, e.g. illness, unemployment, etc. If something unfortunate happens and you run into some difficulty, you may decide to sell property to free up cash to cover unexpected expenses. If you don't have the right structure and flexibility then the bank could control the sale proceeds and force you to repay debt, rather than access the funds to stay afloat.

4. **Easier administration** and straightforward account-keeping – a happy accountant and a paper trail which correlates will appease a curious tax officer. Correct structuring ensures you have a sound basis for claiming deductions by separating the loans of each property and defining the loan purpose.

5. **Stand-alone loans** create the greatest flexibility. Cross-securitising loans will lead to trouble. Establish a stand-alone loan secured by one property only. To finance 20% of your next property plus costs, arrange a separate loan, secured by the new property for the remaining 80% purchase.

6. **Planning!** The right structure can create contingencies which will cater for life's unexpected happenings. Correct structures will let you plan ahead for future investing. Therefore, you will be able to execute your strategy in the anticipated timeframe to achieve your goals.

## Steps in the financing process

So we've looked at the benefits of using debt in the right structure to build wealth through property. Next we look at the financing process – from selecting a loan to building equity, see Figure 12.

### FIGURE 12: Loan-to-equity process

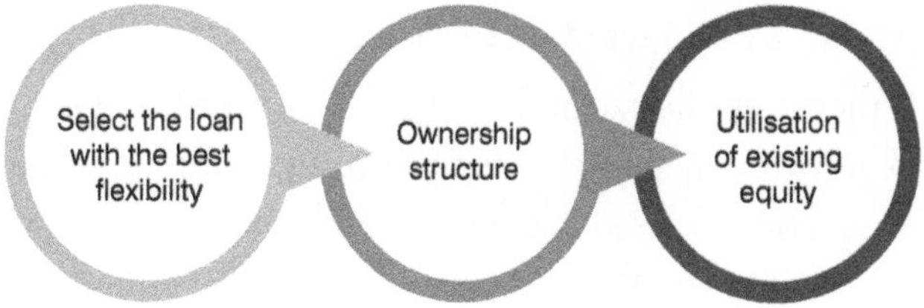

*Step 1 - Choosing the right loan type and features*

The first step is selecting your loan. There are two ways to assess a loan:

1. Look at the specifics of the loan itself, such as the small differences between lenders' fees and interest rates
2. Think of the big picture first and choose the product second.

Choosing the right loan product can end up saving you a considerable sum compared to a potentially small saving in interest rates on a couple of loans. It is certainly possible to achieve the best of both worlds, but it is in your interest to concentrate on your strategy and not on the best rate offered at a particular point in time.

## Example: simple structuring for the long term

Two first-home buyers intend to live in their property for an 18 to 24-month period and subsequently turn it into an investment property. In this case, an efficient structure could look like this:

1. They take out an interest-only loan with a mortgage offset account. That way they can funnel any repayments above the minimum required amount into the offset account.

2. Any accumulated equity could be used to fund their next purchase. And having the funds build up in the offset account would effectively mean that the borrower would not pay any extra interest on the loan.

3. If they keep their debt level high, the interest charged would be fully tax-deductible when the property becomes a rental. This is opposed to having made repayments on the principal of the loan which would have resulted in less interest costs to claim.

This structure works for the borrower because they would not be paying any more interest than if they had taken out a more traditional loan. From a taxation point of view, their future deductions will be maximised when it becomes an investment.

### Step 2 – Ownership structure

As previously outlined, ownership structures bring various advantages and are appropriate depending on what you are trying to achieve. Choosing the right ownership structure can affect how funds are distributed and how assets can be protected.

Let's look at another example.

A husband and wife are purchasing their home. The husband, Steve, is self-employed and his wife, Rachel, works in a full-time PAYG position. In this case, to buy the property and protect their assets, the best structure would be to hold the title in one name – ideally the wife's. The reason is to separate the 'business' from the 'personal' and, of course, add a level of protection. The same would apply for de-facto couples in a similar situation. It is best to have the individual not involved in the business as the sole owner of the investment property. The loan could still be set up in joint names, or the non-owner could act as a guarantor if needed, depending on the chosen lender's policy at the time.

The other consideration might be to own the property via a trust. Banks will not accept all trust types, but family trusts (discretionary trusts) are very common and widely accepted. Say the husband, Steve, in the above scenario is a builder, he could have his accountant set up a new family trust and a special purpose company to act as trustee for his family trust. Steve would serve as the sole director and share-holder of the trustee company. If he were to purchase the property and hold it in his name, the setup could be:

- Owner/mortgage holder – Steve Pty Ltd (as trustee for Steve's Family Trust)
- Borrower – Steve Pty Ltd (as trustee for Steve's Family Trust)
- Guarantor – Steve.

If Steve took this approach, there could be some tax advantages if the property was an investment. Another set up could be Steve being the borrower, and the guarantor would be Steve's trustee company. But, the more complex the structure, the fewer lenders will be willing to back it.

*Step 3 – Utilising equity*

Using equity in their homes to fund the purchase of their investment property is a favoured strategy of most property investors. It is a great strategy to build wealth, but a common mistake made is not having the standalone mortgages on each property. Cross-securitisation is where the lender will have security over more than one property (see definition earlier in the chapter). There are three distinct disadvantages of cross-securitisation:

- It limits the amount you can borrow (because you lack control over valuations)
- It ties you to a particular lender and reduces your flexibility and negotiating power
- You have no control over sales proceeds – they go back to pay off the original loan.

If your plan is to build wealth through property, as it should be, you need to have flexibility to source funds from other lenders who may have better products. Options other than cross-securitising are to:

1. Set up a redraw or a line of credit (LOC) facility so that you can quickly and easily access equity in the property. In this situation, it would also be wise to arrange for pre-approval on your lending so that you know how much you can spend.
2. Use the LOC to pay for the deposit and purchasing costs to secure the investment property.
3. Use the new property as the stand-alone security for the investment loan. Depending on your preferred strategy you could look to manufacture equity through a strategic renovation. Once complete, have the property revalued, redraw the equity and pay back the LOC.
4. Rinse and repeat!

It is important to have surplus funds in the LOC (rainy day funds), along with a long-term plan for taking action. The successful result of such an approach is that you have mortgages secured by their respective standalone properties.

## FIXING A BAD STRUCTURE

Untangling a series of crossed-collateralised properties can be quite difficult. This is because a wrong structure is usually beneficial to the lender as it gives them greater security. Therefore, it could well be a case of having to take your business elsewhere and refinancing your existing portfolio. An experienced broker will be able to help in this situation because of their exposure to multiple lenders and structures. Changing or splitting a few loans will most likely have to happen, and often professional packages will allow you to do this.

It is worth pointing out that it may not be possible to restructure if the loan is 'fixed', because untangling this arrangement will likely trigger costly fees. In this case, it may be best to wait for those fixed periods to expire.

Professional packages are beneficial as they allow a customer to apply for separate mortgages without any extra upfront or ongoing fees. They are useful for structuring as they allow you to set up the optimal structure for each property. Alternatively, you could restructure the loans with various lenders to achieve that optimal balance.

Other considerations you should look at when assessing your existing loan structures might include:

1. Excessive security – there is no benefit to you as an investor to provide more security than a lender needs. As a rule of thumb, try and keep to an 80% LVR. Some suggest 90% to

hold the maximum amount of good debt, but I prefer to be a little more conservative.

2. Interest only (IO) vs principal & interest (P&I) – there is a misconception that with an IO loan you are limited to repaying only the interest. However, you can elect IO and repay either IO or P&I. Any principal repayments are classified as additional repayments. These can be redrawn when and if required.

3. Borrowing capacity – this can vary greatly due to lenders' policies and serviceability requirements.

4. Mixing business with pleasure – if you are self-employed and hold all your property assets with the same lender, it can be a convenient and hassle-free relationship. However, your lender will know too much! Hypothetically you could have a drop in business revenue for a few months and still want to apply for an investment loan. In this case, your lender might just start asking more questions that a lender unfamiliar with all your financial affairs would not deem necessary.

5. Stagger your fixed rate loan terms – from time to time it will be worth fixing the rate on your loans, and when you do so it is sound management to stagger the expiration dates. This will give you more flexibility to review and change your investments over the medium term.

6. Your best chance to maximise tax deductibility is at the start when you first take out a loan. You cannot increase the loan later on, as the purpose will change and this will affect the overall tax deduction. This is why some experts suggest a 90% LVR at the outset.

7. Be prepared for change, it happens – be ready for what life throws at you and maintain flexibility to alleviate pressure and free up cash if necessary.

Above all else, never go into an opportunity with rose-coloured glasses, making ill-informed decisions without seeking professional advice. That kind of concoction is a recipe for disaster.

Now, we have spoken a lot about not cross-securitising, however, if you find yourself without sufficient equity in a single property to make the required deposit for the next purchase then 'crossing' the loans may be your only option. If this is the case, though, once enough equity has been created in the new property you should work to have the additional security released.

## DEVELOPMENT FINANCE

Borrowing money to fund development is entirely different to borrowing to purchase an investment property. It is classified as commercial finance and has two distinct differences:

1. Applicable interest rates are higher, generally, by 1% to 2%
2. The loan-to-value ratio (LVR) will be at 70% of the land value and 70% of the construction costs.

Just to clarify, the LVR can be obtained to a maximum of between 70% to 80% of the final project cost, and this is referred to as the land development cost (LDC). The rest of the funds will be required from the developer and their partners. Some lenders will allow borrowing on a certain percentage of the gross realisable value (GRV). In these instances, lenders will only provide up to between 65% to 75% of the expected final value.

Financing is arguably one of the most important aspects of development. Running out of funds before completion could be a disaster because it can destroy the project's profit potential, or even just its feasibility.

The larger the development, generally the more complex the financing arrangements will be. For illustration, see Figure 13 opposite. This information would be relevant to small and medium-sized developments.

The loan application for development finance is like a business plan. Success will hinge on your ability to demonstrate that all the different aspects are covered, and that the project can be completed viably and be profitable. The plan should include:

1. Development type
2. Design concept relating to the site and zoning
3. Costs – land, building, marketing, purchasing costs, professional fees, etc.
4. Project sales
5. Profitability
6. Timelines
7. Developer's track record.

During development, the lender will want to see proof of budgetary and cash controls. Before approval, a fixed-priced building contract with detailed construction costings will be required. The project's progress will need to be reported on via cash flow and revised financial projections, changes in feasibility, delays, etc., anything that may impact on the risk profile of the project.

Pre-sales for larger developments are required to achieve financial approval. The reason is that once pre-sales are recorded you are demonstrating to the lender that there is an appetite for the development. This gives your lender confidence to fund it. For you, as a developer, it also minimises the risk.

## Figure 13: Factors to consider when financing a development

Borrowing power

- When deciding whether or not to finance a development a lender will assess risk on two main factors: (1) you as an individual and your ability to repay; and (2) on the project viability itself.
- Lenders will consider the security and the experience of the developer and their team. Lenders want to see a track record of success in past similar-sized projects.
- A quality, detailed feasibility study will be required for the lender's assessment.

Progress payments

- There are six main staging payments: deposit, base stage, frame stage, lock up, fixing and the balance of funds is provided at completion.
- Note, the interest can be capitalised, meaning that the interest can be added to the amount owed at the end of each month, and the next, so you pay interest on interest. However, the lender will not allow the loan to go above the agreed maximum percentage.

Exit

- When sales are achieved repayments can be made.
- If the intention is to keep some of the asset, the development loan could be paid out and refinanced to a long-term investment loan. Depending on the profit margin, an investment loan may not even be necessary.

Finance stages

- Depending on the strategy, different types of financing at different stages may be required.
- Firstly, finance could be required for acquisition, DA and pre-construction costs.
- Secondly, a construction loan would cover the building costs.
- Thirdly, an investment loan could be taken out if the intention is to hold part or all of the asset.

If the project you intend to tackle is on the smaller side, for example if you are looking at two or three dwellings on a block, there will be lenders who will consider this under a construction loan arrangement. I know of one lender that now considers four developments on a single title under a construction loan arrangement with an LVR of up to 80%.

To make sure you are across the characteristics of lending policy, and the constant changes, you should seek advice from a specialist finance broker, like those at The Buyers Guide.

## CHAPTER SUMMARY

- Grasp the concept of leveraging other people's money to dramatically increase your return on equity.
- Choose a financial strategy that will be suitable for your long-term individual needs.
- Choose the right structure that aligns with your strategy, income and taxation requirements.
- Financing is a powerful tool and structured correctly it is an excellent wealth creation vehicle.

# [ accumulate ]

### Wealth is what you accumulate, not what you spend

**THOMAS J. STANLEY**

With your property and finance strategy in place, it is now time to accumulate and build an empire. But like all things, empires don't get built overnight. So make a start!

Start investing at an affordable price point but don't just buy anything. It needs to be a strategic purchase. If it turns out to be a lemon it could considerably set you back over the long term. A setback like this will dent not only your bank account but also your motivation to persist in growing a portfolio.

People fail in real estate because they choose the wrong investment at the beginning. They sit on it for too long and it does very little, or worse, it goes backwards in value. This scenario doesn't provide the opportunity to get back into the market quickly enough. As an investor, you need to be looking for, and obtaining, properties that enable equity extraction quickly – especially if you want to build an extensive portfolio. Ideally, you will pull out your deposit amount in equity within a few years. That way you instantly have another deposit to buy again.

Accumulation is not about purchasing multiple properties, it is about building wealth and making money. Create a strategy, carry out research in line with that strategy, and if you are serious, you will need to invest outside of your local area.

Building an efficient portfolio means securing properties that have growth prospects of 20% to 25% over a three- to four-year period, which will allow you to refinance, borrow and go again.

## IS PROPERTY INVESTING RIGHT FOR YOU?

If you are continuing to have doubts about whether property investment is right for you, consider this.

It's pretty likely you'll have a job for the next 10 or 15 years which means you'll have disposable income. That's great because it will allow you to make mistakes (and you will) but you will also do a lot of things right. This is all possible because of your income. Your paycheck arrives each month, and a percentage of that goes towards going out, entertainment and things like that. So what I'm asking you to do is this. Take your disposable income, and instead of spending it on stuff that's just going to be there and then just kind of fade away, I'm asking you to make an investment in yourself. The money you put into property is quite likely going to turn into even more money over the long term.

Robert Kiyosaki, the author of the best-selling *Rich Dad, Poor Dad*, talks about the difference between assets and liabilities. He goes on to say that the poor buy liabilities (such as cars, boats, etc.), they buy things where you put money in and then the money disappears. Rich people put their money into investments – things that turn into more money, like property.

So all I'm asking you to do is divert some of your disposable income into an investment, as opposed to something that's going to take money away from you.

Over the next 10 to 15 years, while you earn your disposable income, even if you purchase just one investment property, the tenant will pay about 70% of the cost of owning the property. The tax man will pay about 20% from tax deductions, and the remaining 10% will probably be your contribution. If that 10% equates to $100, or $50 a month, or less, is it likely that you will be able to afford that from your disposable income? In most cases the answer will be "yes".

If you break down the numbers and run different scenarios it will be better for your budgeting and in turn, affordability.

Let's take a look at what we have already learnt from reading this book:

1. You know your desired outcome
2. You know that you need to create an individual investment strategy
3. You understand that debt can be a powerful wealth-generation tool.

There is a lot of detail in these first three steps, but if you can nail them, you'll be well on your way to accumulating, which is conveniently the next phase of S.M.A.R.T property investments. Patience and a well-honed, diligently applied strategy will allow you to build a portfolio over the long term. This is great, but several factors will help influence the rate you can position yourself to accumulate properties. These are shown in Figure 14.

**Figure 14 – Steps to accumulating wealth**

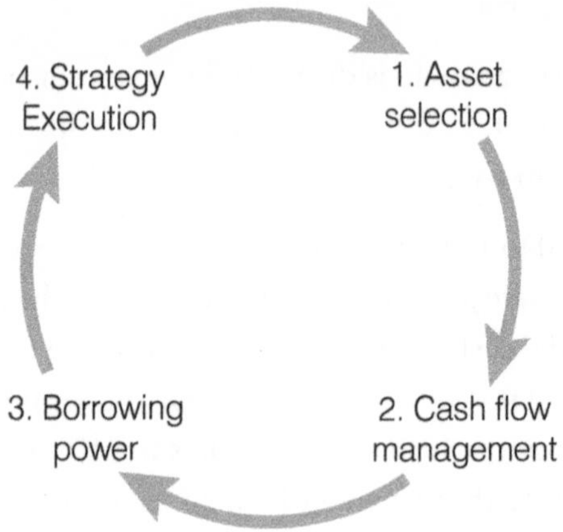

4. Strategy Execution

1. Asset selection

3. Borrowing power

2. Cash flow management

## ASSET SELECTION

Of the many various locations across Australia, only a small proportion will be classified as 'investment grade'. An even lower proportion of the properties available in the 'investment grade' suburbs will be worthy of investment. To make this more complicated, former no-go zones could come back into vogue, and some areas will perform differently to the boarder market, 'counter-cyclically' to the property cycle.

Well-timed asset selection in growth areas has the potential to be a good investment that will establish your portfolio and provide the ability to leverage from it for future investment purposes. Conversely, the opposite will also be true, if you miss-time your investing and select a poor property in the wrong area.

As previously outlined, you ideally want to achieve 20%+ growth in the first four years of your investment. To achieve this, it is highly likely you will have to venture out a little further than from where you currently live. There is nothing wrong with purchasing in your local area as long as it is an investment-grade suburb. Yes, yes, you love the area, but everyone else may not share the same sentiment. If you are basing your decision to buy an investment property on the fact that you can conveniently do a 'drive-by' past the property, then perhaps you need to reassess your strategy, research and education.

Strategy, research and education are essential in property investing. All markets will go through correction periods and the best time to purchase is after the correction – not before or during. Up-and-coming blue chip suburbs will always be in demand, along with the surrounding fringe suburbs where buyers have been squeezed out due to lack of affordability. These should be the areas to focus on. Become area experts in these areas and target the best investment-grade properties you can afford.

Established property in these areas will always have the most value in the land, and improvements in most cases will drive value and cash flow.

---

### Tips on areas to avoid

1. Small towns (with a population of less than 100,000) can cause problems with cash flow and record less capital growth.
2. Mining towns can ride very high in the booms as we have seen recently, but when the dust settles (and quite literally it will), falls in value and increased vacancy rates could be enough to send you broke.
3. Markets that are producing low yields. Expect yields to be around 5%.

4. Areas with an abundance of development land should be avoided as it will dilute prices of existing property.
5. Noisy areas too close to main roads or train lines.
6. Property adjoining commercial premises, such as light or heavy manufacturing facilities.
7. Areas that present privacy issues or areas where there are safety concerns.
8. Areas where generic property will tend to trade between investors and, therefore, won't get the appreciation and TLC that owner-occupiers will give it.

## What about units?

Units have little land value but can be a good alternative to a house because of the cheaper price point, and again equity can still be manufactured. Smaller developments of less than 20 units, or boutique-type developments may be the best options, due to higher land content value. You may also find that older-style apartments are better value because often they'll be larger, have parking, storage and potential for improvement. You need to be careful of body corporate fees and where possible aim for complexes with charges less than 1% of the property value.

Pools, lifts, gyms, saunas, etc., are all nice to have at a property if you live there, but they increase the liability, maintenance and strata fees. New apartments tend to have lower ceilings, smaller bedrooms, poorer natural light, poor car space and storage. The body corporate fees will likely be above 1% as well.

## Selecting a development site

When looking for a development site, it is harder again to find an opportunity that others may have overlooked. Selection becomes more about knowing your market from a location perspective, finding out about the target market you would be building for and assessing the broader economic market conditions. The final condition is most important because by the time you acquire the site, obtain the DA and commence initial site preparation, a year or more could have passed. By the time construction has finished, another year could have gone by, so what will the economics of the area look like then? We all know how quickly things can change in the space of a few years.

The development will need to suit the area and the demographics of the area. How do people in the area want to live? What kind of space would they enjoy and importantly buy? The location is of pivotal importance with any investment, but when it comes to development it's even more important because of the impact on price based on the asset's improvements. People will pay a premium if a property appeals to them and is in a desirable location – not so much for property in an undesirable location. However, development is about cement, sand, bricks, plaster, cable, pipes and appliances – the cost of which is the same in whatever location. While some areas may not be as well-heeled as others, a suitable development that fits the target market and demographic can be just as profitable as trying to develop in an expensive suburb.

Supply and demand will impact property prices. A lot of capital cities in 2015-16 have seen an apartment construction boom. Personally, I live in Brisbane, and by the time the construction has peaked there will be a glut of apartments on the market in my city. Other cities are in a similar situation. While the apartment glut will push down prices in some areas, and more than likely yields too, properties in an excellent location will still perform well. Again it is about timing, knowing your market and catering for it.

If you are reading this book, it's likely you're a budding developer, so the best thing to do is start small. Tackle a renovation or two, undertake a subdivision and continue to build from there. Unless you have the capital, access to experts or joint venture partners, just test the waters by starting small and from there big things will grow.

## RESEARCH

The best way to decide on where and when to buy is through research. Instead of hoping the value of a property will increase you need to *know* that the market will improve. If you can research and find properties that have the right attributes, then the only thing you have to add into the mix is buying at the right time – that is, buying when the market is perfectly aligned with the property cycle.

To get this right, you need to educate yourself on what's happening in the market. Many research methods can be applied. One approach is to look for areas that are at the bottom of a property market cycle, or have plateaued for a sustained period. The key is to determine the reason why this has happened and whether these circumstances will change soon. Buying into a market that has risen quite quickly will mean that you've likely already missed the boat.

Buying an investment-grade property, in a blue chip suburb, primed for high future growth, below market value is what I like to refer to as a 'unicorn'. Yes, these properties do exist but in reality, they are a rarity. Waiting around for a below market value property to pop up means that you could miss out on many properties priced at market value, that are in high growth areas and could grow in value by more than the money saved by buying below market value. So waiting around to buy a below market value property and saving $10k or $20k will likely mean you'll miss out on many opportunities that could well rise in value and continue to be a high-growth asset, over the time spent looking for better opportunities. Capital growth will serve you a lot better in the long run compared to average growth and higher income.

> **TIP:** Don't penny-pinch. Pay for qualified professionals and pay for worthwhile research.

## Effective research methods

There are numerous tools available to complete your research – some are free and some you have to pay for. A perfect starting point is with Google – probably the most popular free research tool. But what do you search for? The list below gives several online free resources which can help you build a comprehensive overview of a prospective property. For information on:

### Established and planned infrastructure spending:

- www.infrastructure.gov.au – information overload but a worthy investment of time if you like to get to the nitty gritty
- www.arrb.com.au – produces transport-related publications
- www.alga.asn.au – useful site for local government links.

### Historical capital growth:

- www.residex.com.au – a comprehensive property valuation and statistics tool.

### Population:

- www.abs.gov.au – for all the charts and graphs you could ever dream of.

### Rental vacancy statistics:

- www.sqmresearch.com.au – comprehensive historical rental data.

## General information:

- *Australian Property Investor* magazine – great articles and case studies.
- www.realestate.com.au and www.domain.com.au – look under 'Rent' to see the number of properties listed in the area.
- Speak with local property managers – general questions to ask:
  - Tell me about the qualities and demographics of the area
  - Is there an airport or are there train lines nearby? Who uses them (commuters or country travellers, freight, etc.)?
  - Is the property type in demand in the area?
  - Who is likely to rent this particular property?
  - What's the ratio of owner-occupiers to renters in the neighbourhood?
  - What do tenants typically expect/want/desire in the area?
  - For how long do properties typically stay vacant?
  - What are the seasonal peaks and troughs?

## Building:

- Visit project sites
- Obtain testimonials
- Ask for references
- Refer to local property managers/real estate agents to evaluate their reputation
- Post on online forums such as Whirlpool.

## Amenities:

- Google maps
- www.walkscore.com.au
- www.whereis.com.au.

Also, make general observations by considering:

- Aspect and outlook

- Natural light
- Slope/gradient of the property
- Talking to neighbours.

For a comprehensive property research checklist along with other free resources please refer to **www.thebuyersguide.com.au/resources**

## CHOOSING THE RIGHT CAPITAL GROWTH PROPERTY

As noted, there are few investment-grade areas at any one point in time, with fewer investment-grade properties in these areas. Hence, it is important to choose wisely. The following are aspects that will help influence your decision when you are choosing a property for capital growth:

- The market cycle – look for areas that may not have grown for an extended period
- Look for property where you can obtain or create value either through time or renovation
- Try to find out about new infrastructure developments or employment nodes
- Favour areas with a high percentage of owner-occupiers.

**Areas to avoid**

Avoid markets reliant on the resources industry. These areas boomed recently and have come crashing down. Resources companies are now also moving towards employing fly in, fly out (FIFO) workforces that live in on-site camps, so the private rental markets in mining towns are not so active.

The falls in property values in these areas have been twofold. First, the mining boom has passed and more and more indicators conclude that it was a once-in-a-generation type boom. Second, during the boom, developers rolled in, increased stock, and expected the miners to reside in the town long term which hasn't happened. A lot of investors have recorded significant falls in their valuations because of this.

Also, be careful of small regional towns with populations of less than 50,000. Generally, the capital growth in these areas won't stack up.

If an area is predominantly populated with investors, then you need to proceed with caution too. If a few of them lose confidence in the area and sell up, it could quickly have a domino effect. A rush of sales in a concentrated area will only result in falling values. Owner-occupiers are more resilient. They don't want the upheaval of moving, and will be reluctant to sell up and leave an area in a hurry. This means there are fewer property sales and a greater potential for capital growth.

It is a cliché but what it all boils down to is location, location, location. It actually will be a pivotal factor in more ways than one.

## FEASIBILITY

Feasibility is the risk management and due diligence part of the process. You've conducted the research, found the best 'investment-grade' property within your budget and there are a couple more tests now to pass.

1. The building and pest inspections – contracts will typically be subject to a building and pest clause. You need a written report detailing the results of the building inspection, any faults, repairs that need doing, etc. A pest inspection also needs to be separately arranged.

   If you're buying at auction, the building and pest inspections will need to be completed before the auction.

2. Conveyancing and searches – the legal transfer of property. You need to ensure that the title of the property you are buying is unencumbered, that no easements, restrictions or debt, covenants, etc. exist on the title. These will be troublesome and limit the future potential of the property.

   For strata title property, your contract of sale will provide details of the strata manager. You should contact the strata manager to discuss the accounts and records of the body corporate.

So to sum up, conduct a strata review of the body corporate (if purchasing units), obtain a building and pest inspection, obtain independent property management inspections for rental appraisal, do flood checks if the property is in a low-lying area and have the contract reviewed by the solicitor before signing.

## Feasibility of development

If you are doing a feasibility with a view to developing, then there are further considerations. You will need to ensure the site has the optimal potential for development and the development is viable. To do this, an accurate feasibility is an absolute must.

**REMEMBER:** The first rule of development feasibilities: Do not rely on a real estate agent's opinion.

Real estate agents are trying to sell stock and maximise returns. Often you will see listings outlining that the property has 'development potential' for four townhouses – then you'll see 'STCA (Subject to Council Approval)'. The agent is indicating that development is a possibility on the site, but they aren't experts in planning laws.

To find out if a property could be successfully developed you are better off to enquire with the local council directly through the planning department. On most occasions they will be helpful.

However, they won't give you a clear indication unless a development application is lodged. Only then will they comment on the submission and how it stacks up against their planning scheme. This process takes time and money and you risk missing out on the opportunity.

Town planners are your real friends in this scenario. Obtaining a pre-purchase feasibility from a town planner is a worthwhile investment and could prevent you from purchasing a lemon. Town planners will also highlight potential problems you may run into during the development process, and which aspects you should highlight in your costings.

---

### Basic checks to complete in your development feasibility

1. Zoning
2. Heritage issues
3. Conservation issues
4. Main road issues
5. Flood issues
6. Water and sewerage services and connections.

---

There are ways to improve the chances of your development's success. Let's go through these now.

### 1. Put a strong team in place

- Use an accountant who specialises in property or develops for themselves. They will advise on structures and tax implications from developing, including GST and CGT issues.
- Work with a mortgage broker to determine your budget and loan structuring arrangements (see Chapter 2 on Development Lending).

- Use a solicitor who specialises in property to check for restrictions, the availability of services and their connection.
- Employ the services of a town planner – encourage them and leverage their expertise and current knowledge to determine what developments councils want to see in the area you are targeting.
- Work with an architect and builder to help determine what property will be suitable and desirable for the location and demographic.
- Use a surveyor to help prepare the subdivision plan and cost estimates.
- Choose an experienced and competent builder to determine costs and help with property selection. This team member can make or break the deal.

## 2. Run your numbers carefully

After all costs have been removed from the potential sale, as a rule of thumb, there should be a 20%+ profit margin. Include the following costs in your feasibility:

- Acquisition costs – including the property, stamp duty, legal fees, rates and adjustments
- Finance costs – application fees, establishment fees, bank valuation costs, legal and ongoing interest charges
- Professional fees – for a town planner, surveyor, accountant, solicitor, architect, engineer(s) (structural, civil, hydraulics)
- Council fees and charges – application fee for the DA, planning submission fees, building permit fees, there could also be fees for land subdivision, rezoning, strata title, development contribution, etc.

- Utility connection charges – for water, electricity, drainage, storm water, phone and gas
- Demolition/removal/site clearing charges
- Construction costs
- Marketing and selling costs
- Insurance
- GST
- 'Fat' make an allowance for contingencies because something is bound to go wrong.

It's probably unlikely that your figures will match from the beginning to the end of the process. As you can see, there are a huge number of variables to be accounted for and financing should be viewed as an evolving process. Obviously, the better the estimating and forecasting the tighter the controls you can place on the deliverables.

3. **Understand the development process**

It is rarely a straight forward process and it can quite often be complex. Be aware of the steps, requirements and what part each party will play. These will include:

- Timeframes – From the application preparation to the approval could take between four to twelve months or more.
- Subdivision – There are five main steps to the subdivision process:
  1. Prepare and lodge the DA
     - If all issues are not addressed or aren't to council's satisfaction, you will receive an 'Information Request' which will need to be satisfied if the development assessment is to proceed

2. The DA will be received along with a 'Decision Notice' outlining the conditions to fulfil for the plan sealing
3. Construction and operational works
4. Lodgement for plan sealing with the council – this will mean that the council will check that the terms of the DA are met
5. Register the title with the Titles Office and the new lot will be shown on the plan. If you don't register the title, the dwellings won't be separate, and you won't be able to sell. Fees could also apply if it needs to be 're-sealed'.

- Building a house involves the following four steps:
   1. Prepare the design
   2. Lodge for a Building Application (BA)
   3. Obtain quotes and sign contracts
   4. Construction.

- Fixed priced contract – the contract between you and the builder that will agree on the total cost of construction, subject to no changes to specifications or plans (otherwise known as variations).

- The construction steps are as follows:
   - Site preparation, including earthworks and civil engineering
   - Slab
   - Frame
   - Closing
   - Finishes
   - Practical completion.

Preparation is the key to successfully steering the ship through what can be, at times, choppy development seas. Preparation and a reliable and competent team should help you navigate the appropriate course with the least resistance.

## PURCHASING AND NEGOTIATION

It is highly likely that 90% of the time you will buy property via one of two methods:

- Private treaty sale; or
- Auction.

You may engage the services of a third-party, such as a buyer's agent or a property marketer to act on your behalf. These professionals serve as an intermediary and close the deal (most likely on a private treaty sale). Whether you do-it-yourself or enlist professional help, it is important to remain sharp in any negotiation setting and be aware of some precautionary measures.

### Private treaty sale

The most common way for property to be purchased is through a private treaty sale. Private treaty is where you negotiate the purchase of property, including the price, directly with the vendor or real estate agent. The benefit of a private treaty sale is the flexibility it offers, including the opportunity to negotiate not only on price but also 'subject to' clauses. Commonly these will refer to finance approval and building and pest inspections, cooling off periods and other aspects which are useful negotiating tools to shift the predominant focus away from price.

### Auctions

Going once… Going twice… Going three times… no final offers… SOLD! We all know the words. But we don't all understand that an auction is quite different to a private treaty sale in that it is a 'cash' purchase, and you are entering an unconditional contract once the hammer falls. A deposit of around 10% of agreed purchase price is usually payable immediately. Real estate agents like to go to auction as it pushes people to commit on the day.

Auctions come into vogue during a sellers' market. Auctions play on people's emotions and vendors hope that this emotional game will push up the result and also achieve an unconditional contract.

## What's involved in the auction process?

Before auction day, if there is interest in the property you need to complete building and pest inspections and, if required by your state, register as a bidder. (Registering as a bidder is required by some states as a way of trying to eliminate dummy bidding.)

> **DEFINITION**
>
> **Dummy bidding** is when a person at auction makes a bid when they have no intention of purchasing the property. Dummy bids are made in an attempt to artificially inflate the value of the property by pushing other legitimate bidders to make higher bids to counter the dummy bid.

On the day of the auction, the auctioneer/agent will have agreed on a 'reserve price' with the vendor. Once this is achieved, the property is technically 'on the market' and will sell on the fall of the hammer. Before the bidding commences, the auctioneer will give detailed information relating to the specific state laws and rules that apply at auctions. These rules vary from region to region so discuss this part of the process with the agent beforehand.

The auction will then commence with the auctioneer asking for someone to start off proceedings by making an opening bid. Sometimes, the auctioneer may make the opening bid themselves and indicate they are taking bids in $5,000, $10,000 or $20,000 increments. Now you can bid in any amount outside of the specified range, but it is at the auctioneer's discretion whether that amount is accepted. You might try and put in a low bid when plenty of other bidders are wanting to keep the momentum going, which wouldn't please the auctioneer.

An auction process is driven by the dynamics of several parties competing all at once. Sometimes momentum completely stalls with bidding still below the reserve price, and the auctioneer will pause the auction to speak to the vendor. The auctioneer may ask the seller to consider a lower price or to make a 'vendor's bid.' With a vendor's bid, the auctioneer can come back and indicate that the vendor has made a bid of $X and that they'll take further bids in increments of $X. This is an indication that the auction isn't going well for the vendor, so the property may 'pass in', meaning that the desired price hasn't been achieved and the auction has been completed. Alternatively, the auctioneer may announce that the property is 'on the market,' which means it will sell upon the fall of the hammer to the highest bidder.

If the property is passed in and doesn't sell, usually the vendor will try to negotiate with the highest bidder on the day to close out a deal.

### Tips for bidding at auction

- Bid with confidence.
- Bid in unusual numbers. People will look at you strangely, and that's because it's off-putting, but it's just another way of playing the game.
- Don't get caught up in the hype. Don't let the agent pressure you and get in your face. There is a thing called 'personal space' – make sure yours is respected.

- Remember a deposit, usually 10% of purchase price, is payable immediately after the auction. The balance is paid at settlement.
- There is no cooling-off period.
- Building and pest inspections need to be completed before the auction, and the contract will not be subject to these clauses.
- Your finance will require approval before committing to the contract as it is a cash sale.
- Don't set your limit on a round figure because it may mean missing out by a marginal amount. Say you set your price at $500,000 but the property sells for $507,000, you will be a little miffed.
- Stay within your budget, there will be other opportunities if you miss out.

It's a good idea to get some practice. Go to a few auctions to observe and give it a bit of a test run. Get to know the whole process and on the day stick to your budget, make sure you have your paperwork sorted, be registered to bid, bring the deposit and bring a friend so you can squeeze their hand, or they can rein in your enthusiasm if you start wanting to bid beyond your budget. Good luck!

## A word about deposit bonds

Deposit bonds are a cost-effective way to cover the deposit on your purchase when you cannot immediately access the money. However, you will still need to have your finance approved if you are bidding at auction. The bond will be equal in value to the deposit. The bond is an insurance policy in that money doesn't exchange hands, and the funds are paid in full at settlement. The deposit bond is a fall-back measure in that, if you forfeit the contract, the vendor can recoup the deposit through insurance. If you're thinking of using this method, seek professional legal advice as there are catches and in some purchasing arrangements they won't be accepted.

## Negotiation

Numerous books have been written on the art of negotiation but let's try and do the subject some justice with a few tips to consider.

Now, in a private treaty arrangement, the typical scenario will be for the vendor to want to sell at top market value and the astute buyer will want to buy at below market value. Therefore, fair market value is probably somewhere in between the two parties' expectations. In these situations, both parties will have to 'do the dance', tweak, twirl and twerk their way around to achieve the desired result. So as a buyer here are some factors that can help you take the lead:

1. Put your offer in writing. Legally, agents are required to take written offers to the vendor. A cheap verbal offer may make an agent nervous, particularly if they've over-promised the vendor.
2. Staple a deposit cheque to the offer letter – doing so will speak volumes and the perception to the seller will be that they are very close to doing a deal because they actually see the numbers in front of them. The cheque only gets deposited once an offer is accepted.
3. Never reveal your walk-away price as the other party will try their best to get you to that upper limit.
4. Don't entirely centre the negotiation around price. For example, state that you need a 90-day settlement in your original written offer. If the offer gets knocked back, you could return with a slightly better monetary offer and sweeten the deal with a shorter proposed settlement date.

> Use the conditions in the contract to your advantage.
> Don't always just focus on price.

5.  Remember, real estate agents want to do deals so they will play both sides to influence the outcome.

Negotiation is highly dependent on the state of the market. In a buyers' market, you could throw in a lowball offer and you might get it over the line. In a sellers' market, you may need to pay a premium. Educate yourself on where things are at and take decisive action from there.

## Buyer's agents

Buyer's agents are coming into vogue because of their expertise in sourcing and negotiating a property purchase on your behalf. They can be a valuable member of your team because it's like having a hired gun doing the job for you. Think of a buyer's agent as a coach. They should educate, challenge and point you in the right direction to achieve the best outcome.

You could use a buyer's agent to bid at the auction on your behalf. They could take a brief, search, find and negotiate the purchase on your behalf. They may charge a flat fee or a percentage of the purchase price.

The benefits of using a buyer's agent are their access to networks and their expertise and hopefully their skills as negotiators. They can also save you time. In some cases, their individual expertise could be of significant value, saving you the legwork as well. Particularly if you are purchasing in a different state or region, go with a buyer's agent who is local to the area and has the home-ground advantage. The critical success factor is to be particularly clear about your expectations; otherwise, you may be disappointed with the search results they produce.

Engaging a buyer's agent requires due diligence too. Go for a fee structure that is performance/outcome-based and do background checks. Make sure the buyer's agent you choose to work with is licensed, and consider checking references as well. Always ensure they are independent and not affiliated with particular agents. Remember they aren't doing this for free so don't forget to include their costs in the purchase price.

If the buyer's agent has his or her finger on the pulse and knows the market, and also procures the property for you, the whole relationship could work to your advantage.

## Third-party arrangements, seminars, property marketers

Property marketers and 'coach' or 'guru' type property seminars are continuing to gain popularity. Perhaps I should say they are obtaining more market share, due to their ability to access new customers through social networking forums and platforms. The digital space has transformed the property industry and the way in which we communicate, particularly with new online disruptors emerging in the property and the financial technology spaces.

New property aggregators are popping up providing online access to multiple development stock lists. In this arrangement, developers are happy to pay referral fees/commissions to on-sell their units, so that they can take the profit and move on to the next project.

There is nothing wrong with this. If anything it is beneficial, as it provides choice and alternative methods to access stock. However, while the vast majority of operators do the right thing there are some who won't. Needless to say, it is just like any other industry.

## Precautionary measures

Price will be one of the biggest factors in the overall consideration of any investment. As a precautionary measure to ensure your new investment stacks up you should seek an independent valuation. You should also seek out a good conveyancer to make sure that the property is unencumbered – in other words that you are purchasing a clean title. All easement, boundary and other searches should be completed. You need to create a no-surprises type of environment.

---

### Three simple factors that could get you unstuck

1. Being too emotionally invested – agents and vendors can smell desperation. If you fall in love with a property and want to shout it from the rooftops, you'll see the dollar signs rolling in the real estate agent's eyes.
2. Not knowing the market – do your research, have knowledge of previous comparable sales prices and do this before making an offer.
3. Not being ready and able – be pre-approved for finance, complete the necessary inspections, use a conveyancer and be prepared to go through the slog of negotiation, stress and worry that could be generated by the process until you've settled.

---

Most importantly, when investing in property, be aware of the sharks. Unfortunately, the property investment industry is not regulated, and the barriers to entry are low. At this stage there are no minimal education requirements for many industry participants, let alone codes of conduct or ethics, nor is there a need to disclose commissions.

It is also a very lucrative industry. On the seminar circuit, often the products offered are highly profitable for the promoters. Be wary of outfits that sell expensive education services and also direct property through their 'mastermind' circles. As a customer, you could be a highly profitable prospect in that you could buy the educational products that in some cases cost thousands. Plus, the property marketer could be receiving commissions on their property recommendations which they don't necessarily need to disclose. A lot of spruikers illustrate their own property success through 'case studies' from 10 to 15 years ago. Well done, but that was years ago, since then they have most likely built their wealth on income from their seminars on the speaking circuit and from selling their products. Do your research and due diligence, check the ASIC register and complete reference checks wherever possible, before you pay for anything.

## CASH FLOW MANAGEMENT AS YOU ACCUMULATE MORE PROPERTY

Cash builds property portfolios! That's why it is so important throughout the accumulation phase. Parts of this discussion we have touched on already, but I want to revisit this again now that you are starting to invest.

Negative and positive gearing strategies have many benefits, depending on your individual circumstances. If you're an average-to-above average income earner, you may find that too much negative gearing will only trap you in your job and cash flow will be incredibly tight through periods of vacancy. There could be other incidentals and unexpected expenditure that will arise.

At the other end of the scale, if you're a high-income earner, choosing positive cash flow properties may appease the tax man more than you!

So if you cannot decide whether you should purchase a positive or negatively geared property, the answer could be both. Each will add value to your portfolio and help accumulate long-term wealth via investment in blue chip property stock. Cash flow positive property will help with serviceability and ease the pressure on your wallet.

Successful investors balance their portfolio, allowing them to continue to move forward. Therefore, the question to ask when purchasing is, "What does my portfolio need next?" Better yet, will be to have an understanding in advance of what next two or three investments you should purchase.

When people find themselves stuck in property investment it's usually down to one thing – cash flow.

Negative gearing is a good strategy if the capital growth is compounding. However, you can't continue to pursue tax breaks because you'll need to make a profit at some stage to purchase again.

Figure 15 focuses on the benefits of each strategy.

**Figure 15: Gearing comparisons**

| Gearing | |
| --- | --- |
| **Positive cash flow** | **Negative cash flow** |
| Self funding | Income losses are the trade-off for potential high capital growth |
| Beneficial when surplus cash flow is not available to fund short-term losses (vacancy periods, etc.) | Losses are offset against assessable income tax |

Striking a balance will help improve your debt-to-service ratio (DSR) and future borrowing capacity. Consider a positive cash flow property for every two negatively geared properties. That should create a portfolio that is balanced and unhindered. However, you need to assess your strategy against the backdrop of your own circumstances. If you are looking to retire, cash flow will be particularly important, whereas to a young, single professional pulling six figures from their nine to five, cash flow won't be the main consideration.

## CASH FLOW VS CAPITAL GROWTH

A cash flow strategy is simple: identify properties with higher rental yields compared to your total expenses, interest repayments and holding costs. Keep adding properties until you hit your desired passive cash flow. You can then decide whether working is any longer necessary.

**REMEMBER:** A cash flow strategy does not necessarily mean you retire earlier than with a growth strategy.

The problem with a cash flow strategy is that the initial capital required for deposits and costs are high. This makes the approach difficult from the get-go because raising those funds could be the biggest barrier to entry for most. Also, higher cash flow properties are typically found in regional areas or on the city outskirts, where capital growth is usually slower.

Building wealth comes from a long-term capital growth strategy. Well-chosen assets can double in value every 7 to 10 years, which is likely to exceed the small higher percentage return you achieve by pursuing a cash flow strategy.

---

### Example capital growth strategy

Say you invest $400,000 in a cash flow property. You hold it for 30 years and it doubles in value twice over that time. This means your asset will be valued at $1.6m after 30 years.

Now, assume you invest $400,000 in a capital growth property and hold it for 30 years. Assuming that it doubles in value every 7 to 10 years it will, at least, double three times. This means the value would conservatively be $3.2m, and at four times it would be $6.4m.

Now each of these scenarios looks great on paper but application of each will likely be a lot harder.

If you're on a moderate income and aim to build a portfolio of five or six properties, it is quite likely you will need a combination of capital growth and cash flow properties to achieve your preferred result. As I've warned you earlier, a moderate income and a strategy of always choosing capital growth property could mean you invest yourself into a corner and stay tied to your job. You could become too reliant on your work to cover the shortfalls. Plus, there is little wriggle room, if and when, the unexpected occurs.

## PROPERTY MANAGEMENT

With the right structure in place, you should be able to survive periods of vacancy and support your investment with your other cash flow. Fortunately, vacancy rates in most parts of the country are low, although there can be challenges in underperforming areas or where there is an oversupply in the market.

However, there is no doubting that periods of vacancy will be stressful for investors, Particularly, if they've had a bad tenant and face repairs, upkeep costs, reletting costs and a longer than average vacancy – it's enough to make you sweat.

You need to be flexible and prepare for a possible period of vacancy. While it makes sense to aim for the highest rental return, if comparable properties are renting out for less it would be better to meet the market and accept a lower rent.

As a hypothetical example, if you want to receive $420 per week from your property and current comparable rentals are set at $400 per week, if the market is slow you're effectively losing $400 per week without a tenant. It may be better to accept a lower rent just to get the lease signed and the property rented out to alleviate some of your stress.

A good property manager is critical for your property success. Unfortunately, property management is another industry with few barriers to entry, and the workforce can be quite transient. Property is a substantial asset and you need to choose your property managers wisely. The upkeep of, and income from, your investment property will determine your ability to build upon the asset. When that income dries up because of poor property management, it will be a costly and unfortunate outcome because it will set you back.

---

### Questions to ask when selecting a property manager

1. Are they dedicated property managers or are they merely an adjunct to the sales office?
2. What is their experience and reputation in the market?
3. How many properties are under the company's management? And, how many properties do they allocate to each property manager? (You don't want your property manager spread too thinly.)
4. How much longevity is in the team? You don't want to have a different person looking after the property every quarter.
5. What area does the agency cover? (Again, too wide an area and the property manager will likely just be spending their days commuting.)
6. Do they hand out keys or handle the inspections themselves?
7. What due diligence is undertaken on prospective tenants?
8. What has been their success rate for matters that have had to go to court?

9. How will they communicate with you?
10. How often will inspections be carried out? How will these reports be presented to you?
11. How many tenants on their books are currently in arrears? What action do they take when tenants fall behind with their rent?
12. What happens if urgent repairs need to be carried out?
13. How are properties marketed to ensure you attract the best quality tenants and maximise your returns?
14. What is the full cost of management including all fees and charges?
15. What is their estimate of the rental value of the property?
16. How will rent be paid? And what are the payment periods?
17. Can tenants provide two references?
18. What systems are in place around maintenance, inspections, and rent collection?

---

# CHAPTER SUMMARY

Accumulate and grow your portfolio through these five steps:

1. Undertake investment planning
   - Understand your full financial position. Don't over-leverage and leave yourself without a buffer
   - Assess your risk profile
   - Put a cash flow budget in place, it is imperative that you know your numbers
   - Have the right holding ownership structure
   - Minimise tax.

2. Structure your finances to grow your portfolio
   - Develop the right structure in consultation with the best qualified professionals
   - APRA toughened the lending landscape and made investors more cautious, and future interventions will continue to influence market direction
   - Avoid cross-securitisation
   - Leverage to the maximum gearing potential in line with your risk profile.

3. Find the next hotspot
   - Consume independent public information, don't take things as gospel and research a broad range of information from multiple commentators
   - Understand risk and have a plan because you are taking on an enormous debt. Learn how to create buffers for fluctuations.

4. Be a creative investor – make money in any market by using what you already have
   - Find investments with untapped potential whether that is equity, capital or cash flow
   - Look for opportunities that allow you to add value and manufacture equity at the same time
   - If the market isn't moving as expected, create opportunities yourself
   - You will need a high risk, high tolerance, high capital approach to undertake developments. Development of small blocks, granny flats, dual living, splitter blocks, and renovations are good projects to start with.

5. Maximise your returns
   - Maximise the tax incentives
   - Learn essential tips for negotiating when purchasing
   - Get a great property manager
   - Avoid vacancies.

Or simply – unlock equity, maximise tax breaks, focus on cash flow, research, diversify and repeat. Success will follow after consistently repeating those steps.

# [ risk management ]

The most dangerous risk of all - the risk of spending
your life not doing what you want on the bet you can
buy yourself the freedom to do it later

ANONYMOUS

In Chapter 1, Steps to Success, you should have defined your risk profile. Now the profile has to be placed into a backdrop of some concurrent forces all mysteriously trying to compete against you. OK, so that's a little over the top. However, risk is part of any investment landscape, and it needs to be mitigated in the best possible fashion. Your overall risk can be managed in the following seven ways, by:

1. Putting together your specialist team
2. Taking out adequate and appropriate insurance
3. Estate planning
4. Investing through the best structure

5. Having exit strategies in place
6. Accepting that sometimes speculation, shots in the dark and strokes of luck will work in your favour
7. Educating yourself and selecting good mentors.

You will have worked extremely hard to accumulate what you have, and it is of great importance that you protect and carefully manage your investments and nurture their ongoing growth. Whether you have one investment property or 100, it is appropriate to have a risk management plan that fits your requirements.

So where do you start? You start by seeking counsel from your specialist team.

## YOUR EXPERT TEAM

You may have developed enough knowledge to be a little bit danger-ous in the property game, but some things should be left to the experts. It's like your favourite sports team, they are good on their own but much better under the guidance of a great coach. Think of your specialist property team as your property coach. We touched on these players in Chapter 1, now we look at them in more detail and in the context of how they will help you manage your risk.

### 1. Finance/mortgage broker

Acting as an intermediary, a specialist investment mortgage broker adds value by keeping you up-to-date with what can be a complicated range of financial options. Ideally, you should partner with a broker who is an active investor, is reputable and has great references. Your broker doesn't necessarily need to be local as you can easily work with a broker remotely.

The big benefit of working with a mortgage broker is that he or she understands the wide range of borrowing products that would work best for trust structures and SMSFs, investing in commercial property, government schemes (such as DHA and National Rental Affordability Scheme (NRAS) housing) and development finance. Working with someone with this range of expertise will ensure the investment options presented to you are the best for your current and future circumstances.

The lender compensates the vast majority of brokers in the form of an upfront and trail commission. Some will charge an upfront fee instead of commission or do both. As part of the *National Consumer Credit Protection Act 2009*, disclosures around commissions paid to finance brokers are mandatory and should be made at the appropriate time.

## 2. Property Investment Adviser

Some investors will look for a property investment adviser, a little like a financial adviser, but someone who specialises in property not shares. A property investment adviser will review your overall situation and help you formulate a financial plan with property at its core. They may refer you to other professionals (accoutants, brokers, buyer's agents, etc.) There are some very good advisory companies out there, but the quality of advisers varies.

## 3. Accountant

Effectively investing in property can at times hinge on how well-structured your accounts are, and your success can be affected by the expenses that you claim and the tax that you pay. An excellent property tax accountant should investigate and implement all legitimate tax concessions that are available to you.

Accurate recording-keeping over the long term is essential in the event that you have to deal with queries from the tax office. Therefore, a good accountant should maximise not only your tax concessions but also prepare all of the documentation that protects you, should you ever need it.

It's wise to use a good accountant because there are hundreds of rental property items that can have a bearing on your tax liabilities. It's highly unlikely (unless you're an accountant) that you'll have the time, knowledge, resources or even desire to make sure you are making the most of property investment allowances. An excellent property accountant will reduce the amount of tax you pay on your negatively geared property and personal income. Your accountant can also assist you to develop a strategy to reduce debt on your principal place of residence or to save for another deposit.

What you intend to do with your property over the long term will directly relate to your retirement planning and estate planning. Proper legal and, of course, tax structuring for your portfolio will not only protect the assets but also ensure you're not caught off-guard.

### 4. Lawyer

At a basic level, your lawyer will secure the titles in your property transactions, across all types of dwellings and commercial premises. The legal advice you receive can extend to the commercial and regulatory implications of the deal to include assistance on tax, stamp duty, land tax, development approval, council regulation, planning certificates, title searches, sewage and drainage matters. Obviously larger transactions will require more consideration and be more complex when it comes to seeking legal advice.

Your lawyer should also be able to assist you with:

- The creation or the discharge of mortgages
- Lodging a caveat or other instrument, such as an easement, which would alter the property title

- Facilitate transactions between the real estate agent, bank or broker and the vendors themselves.

When it comes to straight residential property investing, it's highly likely you will mainly use conveyancing-type services. If you're taking an active approach to property investing and pursuing development activities, you'll probably be using a wider range of legal services, perhaps relating to dispute matters and litigation, if they unfortunately arise.

## 5. Insurance broker

When you start accumulating property, you will need (and want) to safeguard your assets. For residential property matters, you require landlord's insurance to protect you from losses that could arise from tenants not paying rent or causing damage. Policies vary and can incorporate cover for the building and contents, generally against storms, fire, floods, theft, malicious damage and other factors. The level and type of cover will depend on your provider and your individual circumstances.

Obtaining commercial property insurance isn't difficult, but costs will vary significantly depending on the building sum insured, building construction, the limit of the property owner's liability and the type of tenants renting the property. Obviously, the higher the risk of their intended uses, the higher the premium.

If you're tackling a development project, the insurance requirements are rigorous. Regardless of the project, you will need to manage and cover your risks, liability, professional indemnity and workers' compensation requirements among other things. Construction insurance policies protect your financial expenditure during the erection phase of the development, they also offer cover for the developing structure and material purchased from loss due to damage or theft. Because risks vary, you will need to work with your insurance broker to identify unacceptable insurance obligations to mitigate your risk.

Brokers have access to many insurers and underwriters and will be able to obtain the best cover and value for money for your requirements.

## 6. Buyer's agent

We've talked a bit about buyer's agents already, but for completeness we include them in our team of experts here. If you are looking to purchase property discretely, have an independent third-party bid at an auction on your behalf or are seeking to leverage someone else's networks and research, then a buyer's agent could be for you.

A buyer's agent will have earlier and wider access to property coming onto the market which will save you time researching suitable property. They will also be skilled at bidding at auction and negotiating. For me, the biggest perceived benefit is that they can offer constructive feedback on the process, filter emotions and get down to tactics.

By law, a buyer's agent cannot act for and accept a commission from both parties in a transaction. Therefore, there is a level of independence. Maintaining that objectivity, providing access to, and ensuring you don't overpay for, a property are great value-adds in the purchasing process. These are all things a buyer's agent can offer.

## 7. Property manager

One of the biggest challenges of managing a property yourself relates to the legislative requirements of dealing with tenants, which can vary depending on the state where your investment property is located. A property manager can act as an intermediary in the event of issues arising.

Communication with your property manager is key. As we mentioned in the previous chapter, the property management industry has a bit of a transient workforce and you need to make sure you have continuity with the individuals managing your property.

A good property manager should be able to provide previous rental history and other information on prospective tenants. They should take references from tenants and check them thoroughly on your behalf. You should ask for a copy of these references for your records as this makes them accountable to actually check them in the first place.

They will also need to provide you with the condition reports and the actual lease which are central to the tenancy. It can be worthwhile attending inspections from time to time to see with your own eyes how the property is being looked after.

As we have discussed at length, cash flow is king and the life blood of any property portfolio. Therefore, you will want to ensure that the property manager has a robust system for collecting rents. It is best to have rental payments made on a weekly or fortnightly basis. In my opinion, it is too long to wait for monthly payments.

Don't forget that property management fees are also tax-deductible.

## 8. Property mentor

The property investment industry is not regulated. This means that commissions made on marketing property do not need to be disclosed, there's no code of conduct or code of ethics and no minimum educational standard is required to work in many parts of the industry. Therefore, anyone can establish themselves as a 'property guru' and start selling property or advice.

A lot of mentoring programs exist, and I'm sure the majority of them are superb. However, I would hesitate to pay some of the high entry costs charged for expert property mentoring, and I would baulk further if they sold their property as well.

All I want to say is choose wisely!

Mentoring is something that I have benefited from tremendously and I continue to seek mentors actively. However, I'm extremely careful of those who I choose to mentor me. The mentors I am impressed by are also very careful about who they choose as a mentee. You should choose someone who has skills and experience that are different to your own. Education and development are essential, and if you have a trusted mentor or adviser who you can rely upon, you should use them where you can. Ideally, you should be looking to change mentors every 6 to 12 months.

## INSURANCE

Comprehensive insurance cover across your assets, income and life are a necessity. Several main insurances should be viewed as mandatory so let's quickly cover them in Table 7 opposite.

Insurance is something you generally don't think of until you need it. Almost all investors will protect their assets with some form of cover. It is important not to forget about *yourself* as well. You are the reason why those assets are there – you have your disposable income to thank for that. Taking out adequate personal insurance including health, income protection and life policies is vitally important. It will secure your assets and your family's future should an unfortunate incident happen.

**REMEMBER:** Superannuation policies can provide insurance cover so you can also use your super monies to cover some of the expenses.

Table 7: Recommended insurance cover for property investors

| Asset protection – Landlord's insurance | | | |
|---|---|---|---|
| Events covered | Building | Contents | Rent Arrears |
| Storms<br>Fire<br>Flood (check<br>  closely for the type<br>  of flood covered)<br>Earthquake<br>Civil unrest | Structures<br>Pipes, gas,<br>  plumbing<br>Fixed appliances<br>Fittings and<br>  fixtures<br>External structures | Carpets<br>Blinds and<br>  curtains<br>Furniture<br>Appliances<br>Airconditioning<br>  and split systems | Rental default<br>Eviction from court<br>  order<br>Unexpected death<br>  of tenant |
| Physical protection – Life, TPD and income protection* | | | |
| Life | Total and Permanent Disability (TDP) | | Income protection |
| Financial protection for your family in the event of your death | Lump sum payment if you were to become totally and permanently disabled | | Provides a replacement income, generally up to 75% of your wages should you not be able to work in the same capacity due to accident or illness |

*All three of these types of policies can be tailored to your own individual needs. Costs will vary significantly due to your age, past claims, the amount of cover, etc.

## ESTATE PLANNING

Estate planning is done to ensure your investments are passed to your family or beneficiaries, in the most efficient manner, in line with your final wishes when you die. Planning can reduce uncertainties and maximise value by reducing tax and other expenses.

Estate planning is becoming an increasingly complex area as people require more than just a simple will. As society continues to change, and blended families become the norm, a lot more thought and consideration needs to be given to estate planning. On top of this, estate planning can be an effective strategy to minimise risk, if you manage your investments through superannuation and/or alternative investment vehicles.

Therefore, you need specialist advice in this area. A good place to start is to consult the players outlined previously in your risk management team. There are two areas of law that wills and estates fall under, they are known as Succession and Probate law. They are in place to ensure that your wishes are fulfilled.

Let's look at the basic terms and concepts you need to understand when you are considering estate planning:

| Term | Description |
| --- | --- |
| Beneficiary | Person or 'thing' who receives something (e.g. income or assets) |
| Estate | All your assets, including joint assets that will be passed on when you die |
| Executor | Person responsible for settling all matters relating to the estate |
| Intestate | Dying without a valid will |
| Probate | Legal document provided to the Supreme Court indicating a valid will is in place, so the executor can distribute and settle the will |
| Will | Document that details how you wish to distribute the estate |

What you need to incorporate in your will:

| Type | Description |
| --- | --- |
| Debts | Personal loans, credit cards, store cards, and mortgages. These will be paid out from your estate before distributing benefits |

| Type | Description |
|------|-------------|
| **Assets** | Include details of property deeds, share certificates, super funds, bank accounts, investment accounts, collectables, bonds and other tradable investments, cars, boats, cash, jewellery, etc. |
| **Insurance** | Details on any cover and policies relating to life, trauma or disability insurance. |

Some assets, like superannuation and life insurance, cannot be distributed through a will. Superannuation benefits go directly to the person(s) nominated as beneficiary(ies) in the superannuation fund trust deed.

Jointly-owned property is a more complex situation. The property ownership structure will affect how it is distributed. Say it were owned under 'Joint Proprietorship', then the property would automatically pass to the other proprietor (owner). Under a 'Tenants in Common' agreement, you could leave your holding to whomever you choose in your will.

Estate planning is a rapidly growing area in the financial services sector, as it caters for the influx of new SMSFs. Estimates are that there are over 500,000 self-managed superannuation funds in Australia, controlling somewhere in the vicinity of $500 billion in assets – and it continues to grow. It is increasingly common for superannuation to be an individual's most valuable asset. This creates some interesting scenarios on how to deal with it from an estate planning perspective, particularly around how the actual benefits are treated. Payments from a super fund are determined by the relevant legislation and rules of the particular fund, usually outlined in the trust deed, not determined by the will of the member.

If you intend to establish an SMSF, an individual(s) or a company can be designated as trustee. As a member of the fund, you must also be a trustee or a director of a trustee company. If you were to lose capacity, you may no longer continue to act as a trustee or a company director, nor continue to be a member of the SMSF. This would mean that the balance in the fund would need to be rolled into a retail fund for example, which could be costly and it could trigger a capital gains event. Alternatively, you would have previously appointed someone to act on your behalf to make decisions, which we will discuss soon.

> ### DEFINITION
> **Capital gains event.** This is when an asset is sold or ownership is transferred and there is a trigger for capital gains tax to be paid on the profits from the sale. You should consult your accountant if you think a capital gains tax event is likely to occur when you dispose of property.

A level of complexity and sophistication can be built in to navigate through risk scenarios and this can be done by setting up a testamentary trust. The big benefit here is asset protection, because there is a separation of asset control and benefit due to the trust's assets being owned by the 'trustee', and income and capital passing to the beneficiaries. That protection prevents misuse and reduces the risk of any legal action involving the beneficiaries. Other benefits include:

1. Tax advantages – income, capital gains and franked dividends can be distributed to recipients in the most efficient way. The trustee can distribute income to beneficiaries, and in proportions that are advantageous to their marginal tax rates.

2. Capital gains and stamp duty – when you die typically no tax would apply on the transfer of assets from the trustee to a beneficiary.

Assuming you have created a will, before the process is complete there is one further aspect you need to consider, and that is appointing a Power of Attorney. Naturally, this means selecting someone to act on your behalf. Several types of Powers of Attorney do exist:

- Ordinary Power of Attorney – acting on your behalf for property and financial matters only
- Enduring Power of Attorney – put into place if you lose capacity to manage your own affairs, if you become unable to understand relevant information to make appropriate decisions
- Medical Power of Attorney – carrying out your wishes regarding medical treatment (cannot be used for financial, legal or guardian decisions).

Estate planning is an increasingly complex area, and proper structures should be implemented by a legal estate planning professional. If you go through the process of creating and structuring your estate, don't make the mistake of not updating it so that it maintains relevance. Also, don't hide the paperwork, if it can't be found, how can your final wishes be fulfilled?

## EXIT STRATEGIES

Figure 16 overleaf shows the three distinct phases property investors are quite likely to go through over their lifetime.

During the acquisition phase, cash will be king as you try to maintain a steady cash flow against the backdrop of your ongoing personal commitments. Your challenge in this phase is demonstrating to lenders that you are a safe set of hands, and that you have the security and capacity to repay debt. Tax deductions will be an important consideration in your decision-making, together with taking full advantage of the leverage.

**Figure 16: Three phases of investment**

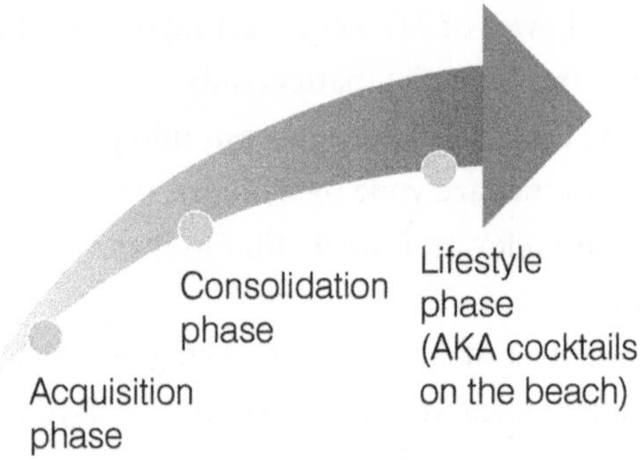

Consolidation phase

Lifestyle phase (AKA cocktails on the beach)

Acquisition phase

Characteristics of the consolidation phase relate to streamlining, reducing debt and maximising cash flow. During this stage, the appropriate structures you initially established will start to pay dividends.

Finally, when you're sitting on the beach with an umbrella in your drink, you can be thankful that the plans you put in place years before are providing you with rewards. In this phase, you could start a new venture, retire early, invest more or do whatever you like.

### Four key exit strategies

The truth is that your investment journey won't be clear-cut. The exit strategy you choose will depend upon the phase you're in as depicted in the figure above. Importantly, your exit strategy is all about minimising tax and maximising returns. Let's look at the broad options available to you:

### 1. Never sell and pass assets on to the next generation

Creating generational wealth is an aspiration and an incredible achievement. If your structures are set up correctly, you would just transfer control of the portfolio, held in a trust, by appointing a new director. In this scenario, the asset never changes hands, so no tax liability is incurred. You're just signing across the controlling assets' holding entity. It's a straightforward dusting-off-the-hands type scenario.

### 2. Live on the equity gains and income

The second option is the simple process in which you would make interest-only payments on your borrowings and live off the equity gains and increases in rental yield from your properties. Once there has been an increase in the property's value, it can be revalued and drawn down by using a line of credit facility. You could then live off those funds. This may be a good option to consider, as long as the value of the assets grows faster than your living costs. Advice should be sought from your accountant relating to this strategy because there will be tax implications to consider.

### 3. Sell and pay off debt

This may sound simple in its application, but there is a lot to consider.

When you sell and make a gain, there will be tax to pay, selling expenses and loans to be discharged but you will be secure in the knowledge that you are debt free – or financially free as some like to call it. Remember, though, not all debt is bad and maintaining a level of investment debt could be beneficial to your overall structure. As with all things in life, if you're drawn to a debt-free lifestyle, go for it, otherwise, keep walking. It is possibly the simplest of the strategies to apply, it just may not be the most efficient.

### Disadvantages of selling

- Capital gains tax
- Legal fees
- Sales commissions
- Marketing costs
- Opportunity cost.

Selling does allow you to access any gains, reduce debt and importantly it can give you the chance to cut off dead wood and create a liquid position to fund your lifestyle.

### 4. Domino effect – knock them over one by one

Start working on reducing the principal component of one of the loans with excess cash flow. Once this loan is paid out, your cash flow will improve again and you can concentrate on paying off the subsequent loans. Just like dominoes, your loans will fall over one by one. This is a decent strategy to use while you're still working full time in the lead up to retirement, and it will produce a steady and consistent rental income from the properties when you retire from your job.

Depending on the initial structures you establish, your ultimate goals and wishes will largely dictate the exit strategy you choose. There are other considerations, but they are largely a play on one of the four above and vary in complexity and risk. Importantly, seek advice from your legal and accounting team to help you decide on the best pathway forward.

## SPECULATION, SHOTS IN THE DARK AND STROKES OF LUCK

Speculation, whether we like it or not, will always play a part in the property industry. Primarily, the blame sits with the investors themselves and their property choices. The finger should be pointed directly at emotion and ill-informed decisions, plus people get caught up in the bright lights of 'incredible returns' – losing sight of the associated risks. Property investment should not be left to chance, decisions should be made after careful consideration of underlying fundamentals of the chosen asset.

'Hotspots' are definitely in vogue and I can understand the attraction of wanting to unearth that next shining investment location poised to boom. Crowds follow hotspots which means the growth there is quick and steep to begin with, as more people jump on board. When the area falls out of favour with the crowd, the decline is just as steep, and if you haven't jumped ship already, you'll be left with a dud investment that you cannot offload because it's no longer in vogue.

Hotspots make me think about Moranbah or Port Hedland, two locations which were riding very high during the coal and iron ore booms, but are now done and dusted. These so-called hotspots have been pummelled, with values falling by circa 70% in a 12-month period.

Property investment decisions should be based on proven long-term performance, rather than short-term speculation. In fairness to investors in those mining regions, the belief was that the boom would last – some thought forever. Like all good things it did come to an end and unfortunately, holding property in remote areas reliant on one industry or employer is a risky strategy.

Money can be made by hot-spotting, but it is reliant on timing, getting in low and cashing out at the top, which is possible in theory but difficult in practice. Property investment success typically is dependent on the proven long-term performance of consistent above-average growth.

## Alternatives to hot-spotting

Don't ignore the need to set long-term goals and develop strategies to achieve them. The following factors avoid the need to rely on 'luck' or making a 'shot in the dark', or hot-spotting.

### 1. Growth trends

When a market has experienced strong growth – 15%+ for two or more consecutive years – it may be best to avoid investing there. The reason is that housing in that market may have been in short supply, causing high growth and high development activity to meet the demand. By the time the new stock hits, the demand may have been filled, resulting in a price correction and a flat market that could last for 12 to 18 months, or more. In this scenario, it is wise to find another market to invest in.

### 2. Population and employment

Look for areas with population growth and low unemployment statistics. Don't immediately look for the biggest 'pop' or spike in recent years, look for long-term and ongoing growth of more than 1% per annum. The same applies for employment, don't immediately look for the lowest unemployment rate. If the general business sentiment is pessimistic, then owner-occupiers will batten down the hatches and won't be buying new houses. And owner-occupiers are the ones who drive growth.

Look for areas that are employment 'generators' such as:

1. Those near the CBD or a major urban area

2. Industrial areas
3. Major activity areas with commercial offices or industrial/technology parks.

You don't necessarily want to buy next door to one of these areas, but a property in close enough vicinity, away from the hustle and bustle will probably serve you best.

One last warning about mining towns: don't be fooled by regional mining centres, because property values peak in the boom due to construction activity and fall sharply when the boom is over. Plus, mining operators employ fly-in-fly-out (FIFO) workforces, who are usually aware of the risk of investing in property located in regional mining towns. Overall, it's probably best to avoid centres that are reliant on one employer or industry. One-trick ponies rarely impress further after that trick is completed.

### 3. Watch for oversupply

Oversupply creates competition among investors looking for a bargain and developers looking to shift stock. Consequently, the result will be a fall in real values. When demand exceeds supply, naturally prices and values will rise. Developers are in the business of moving stock, moving it quickly and starting on the next project. Therefore, in their project feasibilities, they factor in stages and bring the new stock to market in a flow that ensures competitive pricing. This allows them to draw the punters in, or they can undercut to achieve sales targets, or even 'top drawer' the later stages to profit from dwindling stock. In short, they tweak the demand and supply. A 15,000 to 20,000 lot development will take 10, 15, 20 years to sell. And that only indicates one thing, oversupply. It may be best to avoid areas with any signs of oversupply.

## 4. Services

Areas with good schools (both primary and secondary), in convenient proximity to shops, transport and public spaces are always winners. Excellent amenities mean good prospects of future returns on property in that area.

### Quick rules of thumb to apply to property selection

- Less than 7km from a train line
- Less than 1km from a bus route
- Within 3km of a local primary school
- Within 5km of a high school.

## 5. Misjudging cash flow requirements

Not maintaining a property balance sheet to track your cash position leads to misinformed numbers. And as you should know by now, you need to know your numbers! It is imperative to know your incoming and outgoing cash flows. Your properties will experience periods of vacancy when you will need to cover all the costs associated with that property out of your own pocket, until new tenants can be found. By knowing your numbers, you can accurately forecast cash flow through these periods.

Include all outgoings in your estimates and add in a 10% additional margin to cover unaccounted for expenses – and these will certainly pop up! You should have cash on deposit that you can access when the unexpected happens.

## 6. Bargain-hunting

Yes, bargains do exist, but you are much better off finding the right property instead. Bargains are a bargain for a reason. The vendor probably knows that 'reason' but isn't willing to share it. Bargains are part of speculating. Your focus should be on making the right decision, taking the time and having the patience to do so.

### 7. Pricing the property to the market

If you over-price your property you won't attract tenants. Price it under and you'll be leaving money on the table. Therefore, be aware of the local rental market, what's renting and for how much.

### 8. Stick with the fundamentals

As we have discussed in the previous pages:

- Define a property investment strategy aligned with your goals and timeframe
- Be tactical in deciding when and where to buy
- Get the right financial structure in place for long-term rewards
- Effectively manage the property and be disciplined in all matters relating to cash flow
- Get a good team around you and maximise all the benefits that are available.

## CHAPTER SUMMARY

Risk management may not be the sexiest step in property investing but it is probably one of the most important. You need to protect what you have in order to grow. Nurture and provide for it by following these summarised steps:

1. Put together your specialist team
2. Obtain the appropriate insurance cover
3. Review your estate planning needs
4. Consider your long-term goals when devising your exit strategy
5. Make informed and calculated decisions, not punts.

# [ take off ]

### The path to success is to take massive,
### determined action

**TONY ROBBINS**

Life gets in the way. You have the desire and capacity to invest in property, but implementation and management of your plan can let you down. Therefore, control of, and checking in on, the plan to re-evaluate it is a necessity.

Some of the reasons why people don't invest in property include:

1. They don't have enough knowledge which leads to a lack in confidence when it comes to making decisions.
2. Fear about repairs, maintenance and potential tenancy issues.
3. They try and time the market, waiting for the perfect opportunity, waiting for a fall in prices and consequently they miss out on many opportunities in the meantime.

4. They have no time to learn the fundamentals of property investment. If the fundamentals *are* understood then it is the lack of time for the application.
5. Money, money, money! Their financial structure is incorrect, or after a knock-back they are too shy to apply for a loan again. Or it is simply just too difficult to save for that first deposit.
6. They listen too often to nay-sayers who are too scared to invest themselves. Never take advice from those who have not invested themselves.

Why is it that the majority of those who do invest don't get past buying one investment property? Here are some possible explanations:

1. Life gets in the way, and the plan is poorly implemented
2. They have a big fear of debt
3. They have no process to follow.

Realistically, all of these factors, positive or not, boil down to one thing: action. The biggest action prevention is LIFE! If your goal is to purchase five properties over the next ten years, that's great. But what else will life serve up in those years? You may get married, or divorced, have more kids, or spend a fortune trying to have children. You may decide to pursue your passion and start a business which uses up a substantial amount of your resources. Or your career could go ahead in leaps and bounds, producing substantially more cash flow and you are able to invest in more than five properties, plus take holidays, buy jet skis and whatever else takes your fancy.

Life has a funny way of making your best plans come unstuck. Therefore, always be mindful of where you focus your attention, because what you focus your attention on is what you will create.

**REMEMBER:** Investing does not require you to stop living your life, but your life does not need you to stop investing.

Importantly, long-term investment should serve a real purpose, the purpose of retirement. Superannuation was created to relieve the government of their pension liabilities. Considering the cost of living seems to be ever increasing, how much money do you think you would require to retire on as an annual debt-free income – $50,000, $75,000, $100,000+?

Well, think hard. The truth is that 92% of the Australian population retire on less than $43,433 a year. The aged pension as it currently stands is $16,000 per annum for an individual and $26,000 for a couple. So if you don't want to be on the pension and would prefer to have a better lifestyle than what $43,000 can provide then what should you do?

You need to grow your asset base as large as you can with the money you can afford – and the earlier you start, the better!

The best way to overcome a roadblock is by having success. A good purchase that produces gains in the short to medium term will be excellent motivation to rinse and repeat the scenario. Achieving that good result will set the foundation and tone for things to come. To have 'take-off' success you need the right flow to your plan. Figure 17 overleaf shows the property investment success cycle.

Figure 17: Property investment success cycle

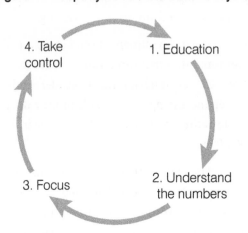

## EDUCATION

Education in the investment property sphere is fraught with danger. Unfortunately, when it comes to passing on property investment advice anyone can do so.

Industry organisations such as Property Investment Professionals of Australia (PIPA) (of which I am a member) is the industry body intent on better regulating and lobbying the government to bring in legislation to change industry practices. It will happen, but until it does, you are strongly advised to proceed with caution. Now, don't get me wrong the vast majority of operators in the property industry have your best interests at heart.

Understanding what makes a sound investment is key, and if something is underperforming you need to learn how to rectify the situation. Hence the importance of choosing service-providers who offer professional advice, service and education, not just property picks.

When you ask the question, "What should I purchase?", listen carefully to the response. If the answer is: "Well, we have these excellent townhouses that have just become available…" and they smile while giving you a glossy brochure, be very cautious. Alternatively, if you get the answer: "First, we need to understand your circumstances a little more and get an idea of your individual situation…" then listen further because they'll likely take a better tack.

What I am talking about is the two levels of education you will find in the industry.

There are the property spruikers who I have already warned you about who charge $30,000 for their 'mastermind' investment seminars and promise you success. Then, there are the professional service-providers who may also run seminars, but they don't have the hype. They typically are property investors themselves, are educated, have industry networks and have a finger on the pulse of what's happening in the market and can help you maximise your strategy.

My preference is to listen to the professional service-providers as they tend to give you more personalised service and take more time to understand your situation and goals.

If you are looking at investing in property to generate wealth, and you should be, you will need help along the way. So, choose a provider who educates, informs and backs their decisions with informed research and due diligence. Ask for disclosure, check references and build relationships. Best of all, take advice and read extensively from a wide range of sources, learn from your experiences and sometimes, above all else, you just have to trust your gut!

## UNDERSTANDING THE NUMBERS

Real estate is a numbers game! If you do not understand the numbers, you will be lucky to get out on top. Assuming that capital growth is a given is the first mistake, and assuming regular growth is the second mistake because growth varies year on year. To generate capital growth, you can either do something to the property to increase its value or have incredible insight into the market for when it is going to boom and be able to ride those waves of growth.

If you haven't done either of those two things, then you're just making assumptions. This is another mistake and one that I am guilty of making myself. However, there are other traps, and they often relate to complacency:

1. Not maintaining a cash flow statement or worse, not having one at all
2. Not understanding or calculating your return on investment
3. Not leveraging unused equity combined with weak investment structures.

A good accountant is key to understanding the numbers and he or she can also educate you along the way. The numbers your accountant can help you with are:

1. Debt to equity ratios
2. Working capital for repayment expenses whether they are accounted for or not
3. Net rental return to benchmark your properties
4. Negative gearing effects on taxable income
5. Financial forecasting on new potential investments
6. Structures for trusts and other entities
7. Record-keeping
8. Set up and management of an SMSF.

Finally, real estate data is also worth accessing. Australian Property Monitors, RP Data, Residex, BIS Sharpnel, etc. are all reputable data-providers. Their data source is the same, (it comes from the government), but each will give a slightly different interpretation of, or outcome on, their numbers. It's important to review it but not get overwhelmed by the mass of information that is available. Also remember that despite the best intentions, data is not perfect.

No single property is the same as the other; and the value of each can change due to any number of factors. Look back at the points we discussed in Chapter 4 about risk management, assess the specifics of the property and make a calculated decision to proceed or not.

## FOCUS

I've said it before and I just know I'll have to say it again: "Watch where your attention is at."

What you focus on is what you will create. If you think and believe that property investing is beyond you, then you know what, it just might be. Or thinking and believing that through hell or high water you're going to build a property portfolio, well then you might just do so.

Investing in property has to be treated like a business. Remove the emotion, don't dwell on whether you like the wall colours of a property or not and concentrate on the numbers, strategy and research.

When you come to invest, it will be difficult not to develop an image of the kind of property you believe will suit your own image as an investor. The trouble here is you will start to identify with that image, meaning you'll concentrate on areas that match your world view, which isn't necessarily the best thing to do as an investor.

Also, if you are worried about what others will think let me share a little secret – they are not thinking about you at all. 'They' have their own issues to deal with and couldn't care less about yours!

Now, you may not identify with all investment-grade properties nor may you identify with the location, but it will be more profitable for you to do so. The best investments are plain boxes – nothing too fancy – that are reliable, constant and consistent performers. Remember, it's a long-term game and steady performers provide security, less hassle and better long-term profits.

So while you may not 'identify' with such property, you have to remember it's an investment, you're not living there! What it does need to do is:

- Fit with the demographic
- Fit the neighbourhood
- Have potential to manufacture equity
- Be an investment-grade property, located in an investment-grade area.

The worst investment sin of all is becoming snobbish about property and letting this get in the way of a good deal. Instead:

- Focus on your strategy
- Focus on the underlying research
- Focus on the numbers.

## TAKE CONTROL

Ahoy captain! You're in charge of the ship and its eventual destination. Now you can either let complacency set in and get lost out at sea. Or, you can take control and execute the strategy you created to arrive at your ultimate destination.

If you are pursuing a passive investment strategy, take control by:

1. Combining an approach that includes cash flow and capital growth. Don't worry what other people say about positive cash flow or negative gearing because you will require both to build a profitable property portfolio. This is important because it will provide you with the serviceability as a borrower and allow you to continue moving forward as an investor.

2. Having the right investment financial structure in place that is flexible, is tax efficient, secured with stand-alone mortgages and that allows you to pay off loans with competitive rates.

3. Having an offset facility. The positive cash flow generated will go a long way to help purchase high capital growth property.

4. Taking action. Once you realise the process and notice the steps are applied the same way as by anyone else, it immediately becomes a level playing field.

5. Being willing to adapt to market conditions and changes that come about in life. It's vital to remain flexible, have a structure to match your strategy and remain open to opportunity.

If you are pursuing an active investment strategy, take control by:

1. Working and collaborating with like-minded investors who share the same investment strategy yet bring different skills or attributes to the table.

2. Investing in professional expertise at all stages of the project's lifecycle. Yes, you know a lot, but others know a lot more in areas where they specialise. Therefore, have them as part of your team. Don't try and project-manage a development while holding down a full-time job. That will be a disaster.

Instead, hire a project manager. If you can't make contingencies for an experienced professional team in your feasibility, then the deal is too skinny, and you should probably try and source another. This might be a case of taking control by actually letting go!

3. Understanding your liabilities across insurance and GST.
4. Carrying out due diligence, feasibility on investment-grade and profitable projects and being able to meet lending requirements.
5. Starting small, learning, profiting, repeating. Gaining experience and profits from early projects will allow you to tackle bigger developments in the future. It takes time – manage the risks and start small.

Rising interest rates, increasing construction costs, property down-turns, disputes, changing laws, regulations and building codes, delays, etc., etc., etc., are all largely outside of your control. Success is about having an active investment strategy and mitigating the risks. Control what you can and manage anything else as it arises. Importantly, don't bite off more than you can chew.

## Take control of your assets

They are your assets. They are your ticket to financial freedom. Care for them. Grow them. Be disciplined to ensure their success. Enjoy the benefits. Pass them on to your kids. Use them to fund your retirement.

An asset that is not typically controlled until a later date is your super. Do you know who your super fund manager is? Do you know what your super balance is to the nearest ten thousand dollars? Do you know how the money is invested? Or even what it is invested in?

If 92% of the Australian population retires on less than $43,433, wouldn't you like to be in the 8% who live comfortably now and in the future? If so, then take action! Take control! Grow your asset base as large as you can with the money that you can afford. Start securing your financial future now!

## WHERE TO GO FOR HELP

**www.thebuyersguide.com.au** and **www.rentvesting.com.au** are free resources that are available for you to further your knowledge on all things property and finance. The Buyers Guide aims to create value and generate wealth for our clients by advising and creating personalised S.M.A.R.T. property investment pathways. Please check out our website or organise a time to say 'hello' through a consultation session.

Alternatively, tune in to The Buyers Guide Podcast which is a weekly show where we speak with industry experts about, of course, all things property and finance.

Peter Mastroianni is an avid believer that anyone can purchase property when they know how. Technology, communication and information is helping break down pre-existing barriers. This has helped the emergence of the 'Rentvestor' and Peter is helping to champion this cause as an alternative method of commencing and securing your financial future. Through **www.rentvesting.com.au** Peter hopes to continue to educate aspiring and experienced investors alike, while providing innovative and transparent property investment alternatives to the market. Again, stop by, there might just be something new that will catch your eye.

# [ index ]